RADITION BECOMES INNOVATION BECOME

The splendor of nature perceived from an altar. (56)

S TRADITION BECOMES INNOVATION BECO

Modern Religious Architecture in America

by BARTLETT HAYES

The Pilgrim Press

New York

Copyright © 1983 The Pilgrim Press
All rights reserved

No part of this publication may be reproduced, stored in a retrieval system, or transmitted
in any form or by any means, electronic, mechanical, photocopying, recording, or otherwise (brief quotations used in magazines or newspaper reviews excepted), without
the prior permission of the publisher.

Library of Congress Cataloging in Publication Data

Hayes, Bartlett H., 1904–
Tradition becomes innovation.

1. Liturgy and architecture—United States.
2. Churches—United States.   3. Mosques—United States.
4. Temples—United States.   5. Architecture, Modern—
20th century—United States.   I. Title.
NA5212.H39   1983   726′.0973   82-18581
ISBN 0-8298-0635-0
ISBN 0-8298-0624-5 (pbk.)

Credits for illustrations appear in the List of Illustrations.
Book design by Carl Zahn.

NA
5212
H39
1983

The Pilgrim Press, 132 West 31 Street, New York, New York 10001

Contents

Acknowledgments

For those who contemplate building a new church, their own needs are of obvious importance. This book is intended to help meet those needs by illustrating how similar elements of different churches have been designed in a variety of ways. Depending on particular situations, some of these ways possess greater aesthetic merit than others. In order to find potentially useful examples, I have had to search beyond my own personal experience. Toward that end, I have been fortunate in having assistance from certain sources, to which I express my thanks.

The Office of the Interfaith Forum on Religion, Art, and Architecture, housed in the Washington, D.C., branch of the American Institute of Architects, has been of inestimable help, for it contains some four thousand color slides of churches built during this century. Indeed, so extensive is that file that I have been persuaded to limit my selection to examples of churches in the United States.

I am also indebted to the literature on church building, particularly to such publications as the periodical *Faith & Form* issued by the Guild for Religious Architecture (now merged with the Interfaith Forum) and *Liturgy*, journal of the Liturgical Conference held over a number of years. The volume *Revolution, Place, and Symbol*, recounting the events of the first International Congress on Religion, Architecture, and the Visual Arts, has been enlightening, as have·summaries of subsequent conferences appearing in *Faith & Form*. The book *How to Build a Church* by John E. Morse (Holt, Rinehart & Winston, 1969) has been most informative; also *Focus: Building for Christian Education* by Mildred C. Widber and Scott Turner Ritenour (United Church Press, 1969). *Religious Architecture in America* by Susan Borchardt (St. John's Church, Washington, D.C., 1976) has provided an admirable historical overview of the subject; and I am indebted to the Commission on the Liturgy, Green Bay, Wisconsin, for its pamphlet "Guidelines for the Building and Renovation of Churches." My attention has also been called to a few examples described in *Religious Buildings*, a publication by the editors of the magazine *Architectural Record*, as well as to pertinent articles in individual issues of that periodical. Superbly valuable for the unusually fine quality of its photographic description of architectural detail has been the two-volume *Pictorial History of Architecture in America* by G.E. Kidder-Smith (American Heritage Publishing, 1976), which includes a selection of modern church buildings against which I have weighed my own predilections.

Those who warrant specific mention include Howard E. Spragg, executive vice-president of the United Church Board for Homeland Ministries; and John R. Potts, secretary of The Office of Church Building and the Advisory Committee for Church Building of that board. This book results from their confidence in the need for it to be published. I thank them for that confidence. Above all, I am indebted to Betty Meyer who, together with her husband, the Rev. Eugene Meyer, has for many years fostered the role of the arts in the church. As my manuscript has neared completion, Betty, currently editor of the periodical *Faith & Form*, has become a virtual collaborator by gathering illustrations, reviewing the text, and suggesting how to clarify my comments when these have seemed obscure.

Finally, to the many architects, artists, photographers, clergy, members of diverse congregations, personal friends, and others who have helped, I also proffer a bookful of appreciation.

Foreword

Do church structures built during the last two decades evoke a spiritual response in the worshiper? Do they serve the functional needs of their congregations?

Charles Jencks writes in his book *The Language of Post Modern Architecture* that architecture must have a signifying reference. The Renaissance had Platonic metaphysics, the Romans a belief in imperial organization—does our age reflect anything beyond a polite agnosticism? Jencks believes that the spiritual function of architecture remains and that Post-modern architects will crystallize their own spiritual realms around the metaphors at hand. Growing out of the tradition of modernism, these metaphors emerge implicit and mixed, in search of innovative and explicit forms. We exist in a time of unsettled metaphysics, according to Jencks, but architects are committed to exploring multiple levels of meaning and perception.

I am pleased that Bartlett Hayes, long an art educator and curator of the Addison Gallery of American Art, Philips Academy, Andover, Massachusetts, accepted the invitation to write *Tradition Becomes Innovation,* which I believe will help lay men and women, administrators, clergy, building committees, artists, and architects to understand the learning experience and challenge of building a church. The organization of the book and the carefully chosen photographs lead us through the structure of a church until we recognize tradition becoming innovation and innovation becoming tradition. We begin to learn to see and to "read" a building. We are happy with good design. More importantly, we recognize that the truth of all our faiths will reside in the structures that we build.

Good design knows no poverty. Too often a church committee holds the view that good design is expensive, that an architect cannot be encouraged to think creatively because it will be beyond the budget. But whether the church is to be one small room or a vast cathedral, good design enhances the spiritual atmosphere in which the liturgy can have an inspired meaning.

In short, this book is especially addressed to those who would build a church. Although it is sponsored by the United Church Board for Homeland Ministries, the selection of churches and other religious structures to serve as illustrations was based on their architectural features rather than the particular faith represented. Therefore, it is hoped that the book may have interest and use for many people.

Howard E. Spragg, *Executive Vice President*
United Church Board for Homeland Ministries

Introduction

An essential argument for the design of a church, or of its related parts, centers upon the aesthetic affinity of the church with the religious will it endeavors to manifest.

One usually recognizes, by its form, that a church is a "house of God." One may also know that it is a house for the "people of God," the congregation. But what one does not necessarily know is what that congregation thinks, nor indeed the inner belief, or faith, of which the church is a symbol. In order to understand what the church building represents, it is therefore as essential for a person to participate in the ritual practiced within as it is for the building to explain itself to anyone who wants to know. Thus, observed as a design, the church structure should not only reward the emotions of the congregation but also excite the wonder of the stranger. Its form and space should somehow reveal the inner function (the spiritual presence of those who participate) as well as the congregation's role in the larger community. That subtle designation of inner and outer essence is what binds a church to the congregation it has been built to shelter. Accordingly, modern churches may be expected to differ from one another as much as congregations do.

Part I   Tradition

Knowledge is made by oblivion; for, in order to purchase a warrantable body of truth we must forget and part with much that we know.

—*Pseudodoxia Epidemica* [An Epidemic of Half-truths], Sir Thomas Browne, "doctor of physick," 1646

A man of letters as well as of science, Browne was concerned about half-truths because, as he explained, they were based upon legend, or superstition, which the science of his day had proven to be without verification. In expressing his concern, however, he defined the process by which science was destined to determine world culture, especially that of the Western world, for succeeding centuries. For it is the essence of science that an established fact is valid only until some new information comes to light that disqualifies the old.

Thus, though truth itself may be enduring, it alters its guise according to circumstances, and the truth of tradition is altered as generation follows upon generation. Change is the tradition of society, no matter when or where in the world. With time, it ultimately motivates the spirit, and, through an affirmation of purpose, extolls the divine.

Although it has been commonly believed that firmly grounded ways are the bulwark of faith, historical evidence suggests that faith is better served by a living society than by the tenets of a moribund one, and that the popular notion of tradition, therefore, should be reappraised. To turn to the past is to observe positive changes in thought. Churches built at such times as we now name Byzantine, Gothic, Renaissance, and the like evince structures and styles that correspond to those different periods. Each is shaped by the architectural "costume" of its own period. In keeping with tradition, therefore, 20th-century church architects need to advance the characteristics of the present time so that faith may endure as a vital, guiding force in modern society.

1

EUROPEAN PROTOTYPES

Before examining present-day characteristics, whatever they may turn out to be, it should be useful to look briefly at the architectural traits of several historical periods in order to see what influence each may have had on the designs of religious (and lay) architecture in the United States. Having glanced at such historical prototypes, we might then find it helpful to note some of the adaptations in America that led toward mid-20th-century architectural innovations.

The Ancient Egyptian Tradition

The form of the Egyptian temple is believed to be derived from a long series of religious shrines that served earlier cultures now lost to memory. Although many of its details have only come to light in relatively recent times, its basic shape has been a significant influence on the evolution of architecture in the Western world.

Archaelogical study shows that the temple interior was composed of a central aisle leading toward a devotional area and flanked by imposing pylons (1). Carved and painted natural objects—plants, fish, fowl, and animals—identified human beings with nature in earthly life. More than mere decoration, these images were vital spiritual emblems, possessing divine attributes.

The Ancient Greek Tradition

The Greek temple (2) followed the essential form of its Egyptian ancestor. Nature was also included in its sculptural symbols. The forest sanctuaries of the then-wooded land were reproduced in stone later on, as is to be seen in the fluted columns (the bark of trees), the blocks of wood at the tops of the columns, and the vestiges of wooden beam ends in the roof above the columns. Such architectural details were to influence the decorative discrimination of builders for centuries to come.

2

< 1

The Ancient Roman Tradition

The Romans were practical engineers who identified human attitudes with nature in a new way. Instead of bowing to nature, they sought to command it. They anticipated the scientific relationship between humans and nature as we know it today. Although the principle of the arch was known both to the Egyptians and to the Greeks, it was the Romans who developed it into a mighty architectural style. Paying tribute to the past, however, they covered their genius with Greek motifs, which were inappropriate to the design of the arch form.

An example of this "ancestor worship" is a structure dedicated to the union of all the gods (**3**), as the appellation *Pantheon* implies. The outside of the cylindrical form arched by an encompassing dome was originally faced with Greek pilasters that served no supportive purpose. Still standing is the Greek temple portico, entirely foreign to the appearance of vaulted engineering. Likewise extraneous were the bell towers, added in the 17th century but removed toward the end of the 19th. They were extant during the early years of the 19th century, however, when the Baltimore Cathedral was constructed (**18**).

3

4

The Early Christian Tradition

Persecuted by the Romans, Christians first worshiped in secret underground tunnels (catacombs). Following the geology of the subsurface, the tunnels wound about without architectural direction. Their chief feature was a series of niches, or chapels, which survived architecturally in later churches above ground. When Roman Emperor Constantine embraced the Christian faith in the 4th century, Christians built—in the established basic style of Egypt and Greece—the long central aisle, flanked by columns upon which a timbered, pitched roof rested (4). An innovation was the bell tower located beside the church to summon the populace for the devotions about to begin. Known as a basilica, the name for a Roman marketplace, the early Christian church was thus identified with the community of which it had become a part. It was a forum, a witness to its own world.

5a

5b

The Byzantine Tradition

Byzantium (present-day Istanbul) assumed authority for Christianity when the faith faltered during the decadence of the Roman Empire. Subsequently there arose an imperious style of architecture combining Roman technology and Eastern mysticism (**5a**). Massive octagonal or circular stone structures were devised to expand and support the spiritual quality of the interior space. Inside the arts were fostered to a degree that highly trained artisans eventually contributed not only to Byzantine culture but also to the reviving expressions of churchly devotion in the West. Viewed from without, the walls of the Byzantine church are material and worldly; sensed from within, the eye is uplifted to heaven (**5b**).

The Romanesque Tradition

Whereas the early Christian builders tended to follow classical temple forms using crossbeams resting on columns, their successors revived the use of the arch, which had been so skillfully developed by the Romans. Because of this, the style has been known subsequently as Romanesque. Unlike the Romans, however, who sought to conceal the arch with an overlay of Greek motifs, the Romanesque artisans left the arch exposed as an element of the design (**6**). The chief characteristics of this building style, apart from its frank, direct use of the arch, are solid walls, small windows, and compressed interior space.

6

The Gothic Tradition

As the skill of the Romanesque builder increased, the church evolved from a structure with massive walls and limited interior space to a more airy place of worship. To accomplish this, the rounded arch was transformed to a higher pointed one. The burden of the roof was then carried to designated points along the wall, which was thus opened to admit light in a way that had not been feasible before. Normally, the light was filtered through colored glass to produce a richly spiritual aura.

But the spirit was not neglected outdoors. By contrast with the unadorned exterior, expressive of the materialistic world, to be found on the outside walls of Early Christian, Byzantine, and many Romanesque examples, the Gothic church proclaimed its presence in the community by means of biblical legends carved for all to see. A sculptured bestiary, along with human symbols, encrusted the stone surfaces to serve as figurative sermons on good and evil and so point the way to God (7).

Because this system of building was developed in Northern Europe, the land of the Goths, it is now commonly called Gothic.

8

The Renaissance Tradition

The epoch we now call the Renaissance, or rebirth, denotes a new interest in the forms of classical antiquity and, almost paradoxically, in the scientific nature of the then-modern world. It also represented the rise of new spiritual values, which were accompanied by inevitable conflicts with established convictions. The complexity of such changes understandably encouraged the construction of a variety of architectural forms within a general, overall style. To single out a typical example is, therefore, difficult. Perhaps St. Peter's Basilica in Rome (8) is as outstanding as any, for it includes the lofty dome, the vaulted central nave, the side chapels, the colonnaded portico, and the semicircular apse, all of which are derived from different periods of the past and all of which are found, in some degree, in later churches in the Western world.

The Baroque Tradition

The social ferment of Renaissance times generated changes in thought and style that increased notably as principalities merged into kingdoms and they, in turn, into nations. It was a restless age of exploration when new lands abroad were settled, new attributes of the natural world discovered, and new philosophies promulgated. A new concept of space was simultaneously realized in architecture and architectural furnishings. The resulting style was more extravagant, or bizarre, than the simple geometry of Renaissance forms. It came to be known as Baroque, from a slang word meaning incongruous.

Far from being incongruous, however, the octagonal geometry of this memorial church is emphasized by turrets and sculptural details projected from the several faces of the dome like the spokes of a wheel (9). A three-dimensional undulating perimeter is contrived so that the space outside the walls is fluent rather than inert. A sense of external spiritual animation results.

9

10

Colonial settlers quite naturally built as they had been accustomed to build in the countries from which they came; along the East Coast they were predominantly from England; in Florida and the Southwest they were largely from Spain. During the first two hundred years of settlement their models were the styles at home. With frugal dispositions, often unsophisticated tastes, and plenty of raw materials in the New World, however, builders developed their own vernaculars.

England in America

Long since abandoned, this church in rural Appalachia illustrates the vernacular hand of an artisan (**10**). It resembles only remotely the architectural nobility of churches in England, the mother country. It is built of logs cemented with a mixture of clay, grass, and small stones. A wooden pyramid rests on a vertical box. Together they compose a steeple that distinguishes the church from similar mountain cabins.

Colonial builders often devised variations on designs published in English pattern books. This graceful church is a sophisticated example of many churches that rose thus upon American soil (**11**).

St.-Martins-in-the-Fields, London (**12**), may have been an influence on some Colonial churches.

11

12

14   13

Spain in America

As with all Colonial adaptations, a local vernacular was usually formulated from available materials and techniques. This church (**13**), avowedly the oldest in the United States, was constructed simply and unassumingly with adobe bricks common to Native American pueblo building.

This church (**14**) is more sophisticated, despite its isolation. Ignoring the Native American pueblo style, it perpetuates the style of the homeland as did numerous other churches built by pioneers coming from Spain to Mexico and then northward into what has since become Southwestern United States. Unlike the dense forests that confronted the English along the Eastern seaboard, the open landscape, resembling familiar terrain, invited new settlers on and on. Some paused as the migration of explorers proceeded; others pushed farther, not necessarily in search of gold, nor always to convert "the heathen" to Christianity, but to exercise as well the human drive to identify the soul with a vast terrestrial unknown. That driving quest has been, of course, the mission of religions and churches everywhere. This church is a nostalgic landmark on the Big Bend of the Rio Grande river. It was designed to recall Hispanic roots and to bring the flower of Spain into a dark, lonely outpost far from home.

The cathedral in Cadiz, Spain (**15**), is characteristic of the style with which Spanish settlers in the New World were familiar. It is unlikely, however, that it had any direct influence on the border church on the Rio Grande.

15

16

The Egyptian Vogue

At the close of the 18th century Napoleon's campaign in Egypt fixed the attention of the Western world on the all-but-forgotten empire. A quarter century later, the decoding of the hieroglyphs brought Egyptian history into full view and sparked a vogue for Egyptian designs of all kinds of artifacts. That vogue was sporadically expressed in United States architecture until well after the Civil War.

A striking example of the brief American enthusiasm for the culture of Ancient Egypt is this church in Nashville, Tennessee, sometimes popularly known as "Karnak on the Cumberland" (**16**). Two "Colonial-type" churches, which had been successively burned, preceded it. The Egyptian style influenced the building of the new church to be in keeping with the fashions of the mid-19th century. A newspaper account of its renewed decoration, a quarter century later, commented, "It is a work of beauty and art, unsurpassed by any in the city, and but few in the country. The walls of the interior have been beautifully frescoed in Egyptian style, corresponding to the Egyptian architecture of the exterior." A potted palm, at the lower right in this recent photograph, adds to the fancy of the scenery.

The Greek Revival

At the beginning of the 19th century Lord Elgin, a Scot, arranged to have some Greek marble statuary sent from Athens to London, where it was deposited in the British Museum. Although the ancient classical culture had been in the public eye since the Renaissance, the attention that the fragmentary, albeit pristine sculpture received sparked a fresh enthusiasm for the classical mode. That enthusiasm was evident in American architecture during the first half of the 19th century from Athens, Georgia, to Rome, New York, and as far west as Sparta, Wisconsin. Church building followed that sweep of style as a matter of form.

Ecclesiastical structures rarely followed the pure Greek form, however. Although the imitation of that style occurs plentifully in civic and domestic architecture, churches in the manner invariably include the anachronistic steeple. A simple Greek temple-style church is extremely rare (**17**).

17

18

The Roman Model

The illogicality posed by the fusion of Greek and Roman elements of design, as exemplified in much of the architecture of the 18th and 19th centuries, in no way disturbed American society, which was schooled to turn from classical Greek to Latin texts as a matter of proper learning. Nor did it deter architects from following suit.

In this stately basilica (18) the Greek temple portico, the twin belfries, and the low stepped dome together reproduce the principal features of the Roman monument, the Pantheon (3), as it appeared in the many years during which the American church was built and added to.

The Early Christian Style

The Early Christian style was the influence for the design of this church (19). The chief features are the pitched roof, the long nave flanked by the lower side aisles, and the free-standing bell tower. Examples of this style are numerous in America.

19 >

20

The Byzantine Image

The architects of the Eastern Christian Empire, Byzantium, expressed the
universality of their faith by means of a circular form. Modern American
faiths have found that concept suitable to express the unity of their own
congregations, although they exhibit no similarity to the Byzantine prototype
beyond the sense of an enveloping space. The more precise Byzantine
influence, however, occurs occasionally in the United States, particularly in
Orthodox churches. The example illustrated here is a modern interpretation
(20). Although massive buttresses were originally required to support the
stone dome (5a), here the exterior is relatively open. Modern techniques and
materials—steel and reinforced concrete—permit the use of wide, shallow
arches that appear to act like springs to elevate the roof.

21

The Romanesque Period

A look to the past in order to formulate designs for new churches in America resulted in Classic, Egyptian, and Gothic revivals. It was to be expected, therefore, that the serried, compacted arches of the Romanesque style would also appeal. The style, as adapted, allowed for both elaborate and simple structures. That adaptability may well have been the cause of its relative popularity.

The proliferation of practitioners of the style reveals the romantic taste of the Edwardian period (21). It also suggests that modern taste as well can reasonably develop its own standards.

The Gothic Taste

The aesthetic impetus to transfer the classical temple forms of ancient Greece and Rome to American architecture was interrupted by a revival of Gothic designs as early as the 1820s. Inventive construction in that vernacular was chiefly of wood, with a corresponding deviation in appearance. Later, built of stone, therefore more authentically affirming the spirit and style of their medieval prototypes, these structures of the Western Hemisphere seek to symbolize the continuing status of the church as a lordly spiritual force.

Typical modest adaptations of the style in America, however, are plentiful. Here a characteristically unpretentious wooden example overlooks a New England green (22).

The Renaissance Heritage

The splendor of Rome, ornate and grandiose, has been plundered stylistically by later generations of architects, but it is not easy to find pure influences in American church building. The style, via the Renaissance, exhibits three characteristics: columns with foliated capitals used as ornament rather than for necessary support, arched interiors, and frequently a vaulted dome (23).

In the eyes of many, the prestige of Renaissance structures has, until very recent times, bestowed a gracious image on church building.

$<$ 22

23

The Baroque Example

The Baroque extravagance of architectural form was developed chiefly on the continent of Europe and does not figure importantly in America except in occasional borrowings from Spain, or, more recently, in the flamboyant decoration of theater interiors.

Rather an exception than the rule, this church (**24**) exhibits some of the three-dimensional features of a European example (**9**).

Part II   Innovation

Tradition is, paradoxically, innovative, because it is traditional for each age to beget its own image. The miscellaneous forms of modern churches will thereby take their proper place in history. The ingenuity with which modern architects have engineered their designs establishes the basis of an aesthetic point of view adapted to the spiritual needs of the present time. This aesthetic promotes individual inquiry rather than compliance with dogma, and bestows upon the spiritual explorer the intimation of faith.

1   EXTERIORS

Despite differences in appearance over the years, churches have always been identified as symbols of worship. They have differed from other structures in the surrounding community. Although the forms of churches vary considerably in the present century, each structure possesses an ineffable character that sets it aside from secular buildings. Several elements combine to distinguish the organic integrity of each. Instead of scanning these elements as a whole as they are observed in any given church, however, it seems preferable to illustrate them separately as they vary from church to church.

25

Exteriors

Early Christian worshipers might have found the appearance of this church both familiar and strange (**25**). The campanile (bell tower) would have been recognizable; so would the rectangular shape of the nave, at least when viewed from without. The thin, flat rather than pitched roof, however, might well have been disturbing for want of apparent strength in relation to the supporting walls, whereas the structural glass, which encloses the space between the nave and tower, might have excited astonishment. Design details such as the rectangular openings at the top of the tower, which echo the squares of the facade and the square glass panes, as well as the use of brick, might have appealed to the early Christians' belief in humble simplicity. The size and placement of the cross, which extends the relative proportion of the space between the nave and tower, might also have seemed fitting. The church results from modern design concepts, nevertheless.

26

Further removed from early church design is this church, in which two separate volumes are joined at an angle (26). The sides of the tower support a massive, commanding cross. At its base are two doors for entrance. Instead of a conventional pitched roof, one slope is lower than the other. At the peak of the lower a vertical wall rises to meet the apex of the higher. Colored glass extending horizontally along this wall helps illuminate the interior.

Exteriors

In contrast with the previous example, the identifying cross rising from one end of this simple pitched roof is barely discernible (**27**). Instead, the prismatic volume of the church dominates the area. The roof extends almost to the ground and forms the simple, unadorned side walls of the interior. The lower, vertical sections of the walls consist of clear glass and are shielded by a surrounding fence. Although the tentlike shape is as old as architecture, well-proportioned geometric restraint is the measure of this distinguished modern church.

This chapel also exhibits geometric restraint (**28**). It consists of a simple rectangular volume enclosed by vertical walls without openings except for the almost-square glass facade flanked by solid brick piers and capped by a thin black slab. There is no other ornament. Gone are the extravagant columns of ancient Rome (**3**), gone too are identifying symbols, the cross and belfry; yet the chapel has dignity, as befits its technological surroundings.

< 27

28

29

Exteriors

This concisely designed, small yet imposing church (29) is derived from primitive domestic building of the American Southwest rather than from the more elaborate mission style imported from Spain. The tapered masonry side walls incline toward each other but are held apart by wooden roof beams, which, in turn, they support. A system of pressures and counterpressures is thereby formed that, together with the vertical end walls, results in a well-proportioned, stable structure. The unity of the whole is enhanced by an imaginary vertical wall to be sensed by drawing lines between the base of the church and the end points of the projecting beams. Moving shadows of those beams, cast by the sun during its course through the heavens, produce a natural mobile mural decoration.

One of the first architects in America to seek new meaning in church building was Frank Lloyd Wright (1869-1959). A pioneering example of his original thinking is this Unity Temple built for the Unitarian Universalist Congregation in Oak Park, Illinois (30). At first, perhaps, one may be reminded of an Egyptian temple, but in actuality there is no direct reference to that style, nor to any other. There are no conventional symbols to proclaim it as a religious structure, yet the stately formality of its mass establishes it as something special, identified with the secular character of the modern community it was designed to serve.

Perhaps it is now apparent that today, more than in any past period, churches display a characteristic individuality of design. Certain idiomatic shapes may occur in more than one church, but never in quite the same way.

30

31

32

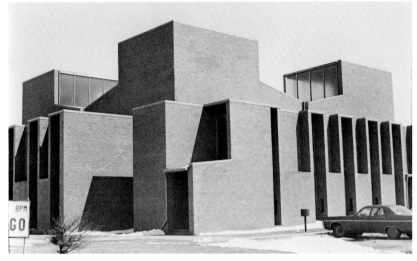

33

34

Exteriors

Like the many-faceted ramparts, turrets, and bastions of fairy-tale castles, some church designs inspire wonder at the complexity of their forms, instead of the stark geometry of shape (**28**). With respect to the interplay of exterior volume and space, these four churches might be considered modern versions of the Baroque style (**9**), although the arrangements of their several parts could scarcely be called incongruous. Rather, they are instances of functional abstract sculpture wherein the intervals of space are as important to the total aesthetics as the material volumes.

In two of the churches (**31,32**) symmetry dominates the external view, as well as the interior space, which should necessarily conform. In the others (**33,34**), the exterior follows the interwoven interior requirements of space and light. None betrays any direct historical precedent. Each is virtually unique in its modern appearance.

35

36

The springlike arches noted in the Greek Orthodox church (20) occur also in this example of a rotund church (35). On three conical levels, the circular succession of arches welcomes the congregation from all quarters and from all levels of life. The design is symbolic and functional, independent of idioms of the past, bearing witness to the religious convictions of the present.

Tradition may have influenced the design of this church (36) a little more than that of the previous example, but very little. The arched volumes of the nave and transept are ingeniously interlocked within a quadrilateral, almost cubical form. Above, graceful arches orient the cupola to the four points of the compass, shedding the light of the globe upon the interior. Because the church is small it is dwarfed by larger buildings nearby, and one comes upon it the first time with some surprise. Its proportions are majestic, however, and with a more careful look the church assumes an eminence that overshadows the buildings of lesser architectural merit.

38

37

Exteriors

This example of a round church (37) designed for a minimum budget is interesting on two counts. First, it is constructed on what was once Native American territory. Instead of following early Spanish mission style, the architect has chosen a form reminiscent of the characteristic Native American shelter, the tepee or wickiup. Second, revealed metal trusses form a structural image that identifies the church as serving a modern community.

In the previous instance metal trusses were joined at an apex to support an inner dome that extended to the ground. In this case (38) trusses are tied together, like the spokes of a wheel, by the weight of the roof suspended from them. The results of the two different methods of modern architectural engineering on the devotional interiors are illustrated elsewhere (113, 129).

39

Exteriors

This synagogue (**39**) is a landmark in its community because of its vast arches. The circular retaining wall is without ornament. The entire structure is an exercise in basic geometry whose simplicity disassociates it from the stylistic grandeur of the past. It is specifically modern and invokes its own prestige.

Perhaps the simplest of round churches is the small nondenominational chapel at the Massachusetts Institute of Technology (**40a**). It is surrounded by a shallow trench or moat, which sets it apart from its mundane environment (**40b**). Built into the arches at the base are tiny windows to admit light reflected from the ripples of water. The wall of the interior is thus dimly illuminated as if by flickering candles (**40c**).

40a

40b

40c

41a

Exteriors

In contrast to the universal role of the chapel at the Massachusetts Institute of Technology is the function of the three chapels representing different faiths at Brandeis University (**41a**). Seen from without, all are similar, signifying a communality of worship. The interiors vary, however, with respect to furnishings that celebrate the particulars of each faith. Thus Protestant (**41b**), Catholic (**41c**), and Jewish (**41d**) chapels stand side by side, all possessing a common purpose but, like three similar but different members of a family, each possessing its own personality.

41b

41c

41d

42a

Exteriors

This Mormon meeting house (**42a**) is unlike other temples or tabernacles erected by that church because of its form, which consists of a perceptive integration of shed-shaped volumes. External features—such as the "window" embrasures, designed to impart character to what would be otherwise a stark wall; the vertical accent of the bell tower, which interrupts the horizontally stretched facade; and the recessed entrance that gives depth to that facade—are all emphasized by particulars of brickwork that vary in texture to punctuate structural boundaries. They must be noticed in detail to be appreciated (**42b**). Even sunlight and shadow resulting from the interplay of volumes and surfaces contribute to the sculpturesque coordination of the building. In material terms the meeting house is the embodiment of the close-knit social composition of the Mormon community.

42b

Religious ritual and drama have never been very far apart, and there have been times in human history when they were intrinsically the same, from the performances of primitive tribes on through the years of classical history, even—less commonly—to the present time.

In an attempt to describe the peculiar appearance of this synagogue (43) several adjectives come to mind—theatrical, fanciful, grotesque, weird, mystical. Now, if the word mystical may be allowed, the affinity between drama and liturgy is joined, with this synagogue as an architectural example.

Although the facade may be startling, indeed disturbing, to those unaccustomed to what seems to be a disorderly array of shapes, a closer look will show that there is a geometric pattern stabilizing the dynamic forms. For example, the irregular window embrasures balance each other on either side of the vertical shaft that occupies the center, the outline of which reveals the bima (altar) within. The apparently aimless shapes that define the compartments of the windows are not only consistent with the larger shapes of the facade but provide "punctuation" for the colored glass windows as they are observed from within, looking out (114, 154). The entire structure is a block, a quadrangular volume of which the upright walls and long flat roof are the precise surfaces. In short, the structure is organically strict, testimony to the harmony of the varied ceremonies it was designed to celebrate.

43

COMPONENT PARTS

In the minds of many churchgoers a church should be identified by a distinguishing emblem, whether it be the entrance, the roof, the steeple that rises majestically over it, or the belfry, which may be incorporated within the steeple or stand as an independent unit. Although none of these components may actually be necessary to identify a church, to look at their differing designs is to understand how potentially flexible are the decisions of both architect and church building committee.

Entrance

How to enter a church may not seem to pose too difficult a problem, at least to the laity, who are more interested in what transpires within than how to get there. In earlier times the entrances to most churches were in the front facade, although side doors were often used as well. Such entrances called, however, for a rigid design of interior space.

The problem of how to achieve flexibility, both of access and for interior activities, has become one of the modern architect's keenest concerns. Here (**44**) the steeple and belfry are economically used as an entrance, leaving more interior space for other uses.

< **44**

45a

45b

Component Parts, Entrance

With respect to the free-standing belfry, the design of this church (**45a**) recalls the look of Early Christian churches (**4**). Furthermore, the design identifies what is taking place within. Three forms—the vertical shaft of the belfry, the horizontal boxlike shape of the nave, and the cylindrical exterior of the apse—explicitly define (as seen from without) the separate functions of the interior. Moreover, the delicate delineation of the portico at the middle of the nave (**45b**) is a gracious sign to welcome the congregation into the bosom of the church.

Perhaps a similar welcome is extended to the children who approach this chapel (**46**). The diminutive roof over the entrance repeats the shape of the motherly, brooding, overhanging roof above. Thus the doorway beckons the small, while the main roof offers shelter for all.

46

47

Component Parts, Entrance

Most modern churches are built in accordance with programs that are carefully formulated by discussions between the architect and committees appointed by the congregation.

The program for this church (**47**) required good lighting and good visibility, for the members of the congregation are deaf. The site chosen was in a residential neighborhood, and it was agreed that the design should be modest in keeping with the surroundings. The architect thoughtfully planned access to the entrance between two full-grown trees, like natural pillars, beyond which a bridge was constructed leading to the doors of the church. Built on an "island," the church thus affords a semiprivate environment for relaxation and comfort. Both the belfry and the steeple consist solely of open wooden frames conforming to the limbs of the overhanging trees. It is the adroitly conceived entrance, however, that introduces one to the essential nature of the church.

48

For the tastes of many people, a cathedral should properly be designated by a familiar steeple or two and/or a "suitable" bell tower. These would identify the building beyond a doubt, and would also indicate the location of the entrance, embellishing it as well.

Contrarily, the entrance to this cathedral (**48**) is shown by the gigantic colored glass wall confronting whomever approaches. The image of St. Paul speaks to the passerby much as the vivid cathedral windows of the 15th and 16th centuries spoke to the citizens of those days. Then, however, the glass was "readable" only within the dim, vaulted sanctuary. Here it is emblazoned to address the modern world without. It is an astounding and unique entrance.

49

Component Parts, Entrance

Situated at a corner of a busy intersection on the edge of a diminutive municipal park in downtown Boston is the Church of All Nations (**49**). A large brick cross modestly stands out from the blank walls near the entrance and explains the purpose of the building to hurrying motorists who, more than likely, have no time to stop, much less find a place to park. The utter austerity of the entrance denotes the silence and seclusion from urban turbulence that can be anticipated within.

Although, on occasion, a church entrance should be unobtrusive to allow the structure to dominate the design, there are other times when it seems more appropriate for the entrance to provide an emphatic introduction to the building (**50**). In the latter case the entrance is like the title of a poem that prepares the reader for the poem's message. Or, to change the simile, it is like the overture to an opera. This bold entrance is a well-orchestrated overture to the composition of the temple. Its design is symbolic, representing the shape of the open Torah, the Hebrew book of divine knowledge.

50 >

52

Roof

Perhaps it is not too far-fetched to liken the lines of this high-pitched, thrusting roof (51) to a person who, with arms upraised, fingers touching, gestures dramatically forward. In this dynamic sense the apex serves in lieu of a steeple to signal the presence of the church. In a different context the apex resembles the prow of a ship—an extension of the nave, or vessel, of the church. At all events, it is an example of how a single architect, Frank Lloyd Wright, exercised his versatility (20, 30) by organizing forms suitable for the particular congregation that chose him.

The high pitch of the roof line of this church (52) may be compared with that of the previous example, but the comparison ends there. The tapering vertical wall, shaped like the spruce trees nearby, is defined by the wooden roof. The latter is supported by stout wooden beams visible from without as well as from within. The beams are planted firmly in the ground in series, like a row of figures, legs astride. The wooden cross identifies the church. No steeple, no belfry is needed. Set off from the stone surface against which it is placed, the cross completes the sense of structure and stability.

51

53

Component Parts, Roof

Gables produce a rhythm to articulate churches, whether round, square, or rectangular. A rhythmic series possesses a unity of its own, which is, perhaps, why multiple gables have found favor in numerous examples of modern church architecture. This structure has become popularly known as the "praying hands" church because of the staccato pinnacles that form its roof (**53**).

Like a baldachin, a flat roof covers the entire structure of this Jewish Center (**54**). The ceremonial associations conveyed by the flat form of the panoply are thus transmitted to the center as a whole and lend a corresponding dignity to it.

Somewhat similar in technical principle to the Jewish Center (**54**) this Catholic church presents a wholly different impression (**55**). The extensive, heavy mass of the roof projects far beyond the lower walls, like wings spread from the body of an airplane. In this respect the roof almost appears to be airborne. The band of clear glass that separates the roof from the basic structure contributes to the analogy—especially from within, where the aura of light on all sides, reminiscent of Byzantine architecture (**5b**), overcomes the ponderous roof overhead, intimating that the cloak of heaven hovers close by.

54

55

56

Component Parts, Roof

If a flat roof seems desirable for budget or other considerations, it need not necessarily be horizontal. This chapel is an example (56). The slope of the roof recalls the Colorado mountain slopes in the background, as does the top of the free-standing, truncated belfry. The roof line above the glass wall is like the upper lid of an open eye communing with the natural magnificence of the valley below. (See frontispiece.)

In this instance (57) a flat roof has wisely been avoided; nestled in a cluster of tall, flat-roofed apartment buildings, the synagogue would seem puny by comparison if it resembled them in the slightest way. On the contrary, corduroy-textured concrete differentiates it from the brick of the surrounding structures, as well as from the slick metal surface of the omnipresent automobile. The basic forms are imposing despite their small size. The building is scarcely larger than the swings and jungle gyms in the children's playground adjacent to it. Unlike the two previous examples, there are no visible ritualistic shapes to impart dignity to the exterior. Rather, the interlocking walls are determined by the religious and social needs within. And the roof plays no role at all in the exterior design, for it is invisible.

57

58

59

60

61

Component Parts, Roof

Evidently, the style of the roof is, to some extent, a measure of the "personality" of each church. A church roof need not necessarily be straight like a tent, nor gabled like miniature mountain peaks; it can be shaped in a variety of ways and yet furnish the shelter and the spiritual image required of it, as these curved roofs illustrate (**58, 59, 60**).

Atypically, the roof of this church (**61**) incorporates a considerable expanse of glass, the purpose of which is to admit solar energy. Unlike the images filtered by familiar stained glass, the solar presence is unobserved yet sensed from within. The "steeple" contains the equipment needed to provide proper technical absorption and distribution of the energy.

62

Component Parts, Roof

The ultimate in designing a church roof is to open the church to heaven, as was done in this unique instance (**62**). A brick wall encloses a paved court on which the congregation gathers around a pear-shaped abstract figure of the Virgin (**134**). A huge complementary grooved wooden dome shelters the statue, while the congregation stands humbly exposed to the elements.

63

64

Steeple

In the opinion of many, steeples or their substitutes are still desirable signs to identify a church. Two instances are illustrated here.

The interlocking volumes of the first one (**63**), composed of sharply articulated flat planes, permit the projection of one of the volumes above the rest resulting in a steeple-like symbol. The interweaving curved planes of the other (**64**) produce a similar result. In both buildings the objective was to construct a dignified church that would, nevertheless, possess its own individuality. With respect to "steepledom," the greatest external difference between them is the use of curved lines in one and straight ones in the other.

65

Component Parts, Steeple   When the design of a church permits the inclusion of a more traditional steeple, striking monuments result from modern creative ingenuity. The lower shape of this church (**65**) is visually the base of the steeple as well as the house of the church. The steeple surges up, but is restrained by the base.

The base of this church (**66**) is more like a launching pad for the heavenward-aspiring steeple.

Distinctly different from the others, this church (**67**) is surmounted by an abbreviated, figurative steeple. Instead, the body of the church is itself a steeple, as it becomes transformed vertically at three levels.

66

67

68

Component Parts, Steeple   The next five churches are alike in several respects: all are rural, all are located in wooded areas, and all employ wood to advantage. All are relatively small. The interiors of all more than justify the appearances of the exteriors. One (68), situated in a clearing overlooking an inlet on the coast of Maine, is ringed by a low wall of local granite. Within the terrace a well-kept lawn and simple flower beds provide the transition from the natural unkempt terrain without to the precinct of the church. The church itself, constructed of local wood, is surmounted by a squat belfry-steeple oriented to the four main directions of the compass. Another (69), is built on a sandy knoll on Cape Cod, Massachusetts, among scrub pines that provide a natural botanical setting. Its belfry-steeple rests on stilts above the roof, like a pilgrim watchtower. The separation of belfry from roof allows light to fall directly on the altar—a distinctive contribution to the rustic yet sophisticated spiritual atmosphere of the interior (120). Another (70) is in a shady grove in a residential subdivision of Hartford, Connecticut. As with the preceding examples, it consists of a mixture of stone and natural wood. Its shape is approximately square. The roof, sloping from four sides, is punctuated by nine low wooden "chimneys" that permit sunlight to illuminate the interior with a discreet glow. The chimney turrets are not steeples, nor belfries, yet they command attention and assert the otherwise unassuming existence of a suburban church. The fourth (71), located in the wooded outskirts of Atlanta, Georgia, differs to the extent that the light falling on the congregation is admitted through several dormers, whereas light illuminating the bima is received from its own tower. Like the previous four examples, the mixed stone and wood design of the church in Florida (72) is consistent with the wooded area around it. A truncated cupola caps the sloping sides of the roof. In all these examples the nearby trees and songs of the birds invoke the blessing of nature.

69

70

75

71

72

73

Component Parts, Steeple

These two churches (**73, 74**) are similar in that each is shaped like a square or Greek cross and the front facade of each features a narrow vertical window extending to the roof. The hollow shaft of the window accentuates the center of each facade, as a steeple might do in a material way. Thus, in a sense, both churches possess a ''negative steeple,'' which is positive as an architectural device nonetheless.

74

75

Component Parts, Steeple

Depending on the wishes of a congregation, an architect may be requested to consider the incorporation of a steeple as an element of the church that will recall the images of many "traditional" American 18th- and 19th-century churches. A steeple was constructed near the entrance to this church to symbolize its New England situation (75). After several years a storm destroyed it, and the congregation has not felt the need to reconstruct it.

Belfry

A belfry differs from a steeple in that bells may be suspended in any kind of architectural shape, whereas a steeple, which may or may not contain bells, is an elongated vertical structure, normally surmounting a church roof.

There are times when a belfry may be most effective as a part of the church building. In this example (**76**) sloping roofs culminate in a screenlike wall within which the bells hang. The form of the belfry is directly related to the form of the church.

A belfry independent of the body of a church is not new in the evolution of church architecture (**4**). One as far removed from the church as this one is (**77**) seems to be a more recent innovation, however. There is a reason here, perhaps, for the belfry takes its dignified place in contrast with the many roadside signs intended to catch the eye of the passing motorist.

78

Component Parts, Belfry

This chapel is built on a seacoast promontory (**78**). A respect for nature was the spiritual motivation for its existence. To make the most of the site, the architect erected a redwood skeleton to support glass walls. Thus, humanity inside and nature outside are at one. Lest this roadside shrine be construed to be no more than a secular observation post, a belfry was constructed, using stone to contrast with the fragility of glass. To place it too close to the glass seemed insensitive, however, so it was located at a distance. The quadrilateral stone bell tower becomes the visual as well as the tonal antithesis of the chapel.

A somewhat similar problem arose in the planning of this exotic church, likewise consisting of a great deal of glass (**79a**). The exterior is apparently symbolic, for the form of the church resembles that of a fish, an early Christian symbol. As an afterthought, a memorial carillon belfry was constructed close by (**79b**).

79a

79b

80

Component Parts, Belfry·

Innovation does not necessarily imply that objects, or the forms of which they are composed, are wholly new in conception. Indeed, more commonly, a new object may be formed by putting together two or more known elements in an unfamiliar way. Doing so is the process of the engineering sciences. The dome of this modern Orthodox Christian church (80) reflects the Byzantine influence (5a); the bell tower stands attached to the church, as an Early Christian bell tower often was. Yet neither of those early styles would have looked like this handsomely articulated combination devised by a modern architect.

The arrangement of the bells that ring out the presence of a church may be appropriately playful. Although the structural support of these bells is actually immovable, they appear to be suspended upon a hinged panel opening from a music box (81). By this simple, imaginative architectural device the casual passerby is summoned to ask what transpires within.

81 >

82

Component Parts, Belfry

Without resorting to bombast or ostentation, an architect may be sensitive to the importance of pageantry when designing a church. Just as vestments contribute to the role of the clergy within a church, the architectural "robes" that enfold the bells of this church are an effective costume (82). Were these bells to be perched nakedly upon the rectangular entrance, without flanking walls or backdrop, they would appear irrelevant to the rest of the building. Here, they are visually and acoustically a part of the proscenium.

Splendidly different from any other example, the belfry of this church arches over the entrance to summon the faithful, both visibly and by sound (83). Like a processional banner, it proclaims the ritual that may be anticipated upon entering. The circular texture of the facade provides a fitting background by suggesting the flare of trumpets to herald the significance of the edifice.

83

3   SITE

Formerly, the geography of the land where a church was to be built had little effect on its appearance, which generally conformed to the prevailing idiom of the time.

Today, on the contrary, many architects and congregations believe that a new church should be designed in a way appropriate to the landscape, or site, available. In this way the church becomes identified with its location and with the community it is intended to serve. Thus its form depends in no small degree on where it is built—upon the "lay of the land" and upon the materials suitable to both.

Ultimately, finding a dignified, economical, and geographically convenient plot of land for a new church is no small challenge to a building committee. To persuade a congregation to accept a location that at first glance seems unacceptable, however, is the aesthetic opportunity of both the committee and its chosen architect.

84

This church rises from the open Minnesota tableland like an ancient temple (**84**). It would lose its effectiveness in a densely built area surrounded by a multitude of urban buildings. Sensitive to the relative isolation, the architect has made use of it.

The architect has taken advantage of the terrain in planning this church (**85**). It would have been technically simple to have leveled the ground to accommodate a standard plan, but he chose to design a church adapted to the slope. He also took account of the intersecting hillside roads that limit the plot. The view across the valley toward the distant mountains determined the orientation of the church. By contemplating the distance beyond, the congregation is inspired to empathize with nature.

The design of this church (**86**) is a matter of economic convenience. The sharp drop of the land was not appealing, so its value was low. By means of imaginative engineering the architect was able to design a church for unwanted land. A church budget may often benefit from the astuteness of an experienced architect.

85

86

87a

87b

Site

Amid the commercial animation of city life, the architectural possibilities of this site were strictly defined. Some thought was given to building the new church atop the neighboring skyscraper (**87a**). This was abandoned as a location, however, as being too remote from those whom the church hoped to attract. A glass church to match the skyscraper would have been insignificant. As it now stands, the skyscraper in a sense becomes the steeple of the church (**87b**).

Occasionally religious structures built in relatively open areas have been all but smothered, as time passed, by city structures that have grown up around them.

Here, the condition was reversed (**88**). An empty lot was available, but no surrounding land. The narrow space precluded satisfactory conventional treatment; the architect was challenged to design a building that would not appear to be compressed by its commercial neighbors.

The solution resembles a gigantic horizontal scroll, partly unwound, which visually thrusts against the walls of the adjacent buildings as if to hold them back. Instead of looking crowded, the design seems to allow ample room for the activities of the synagogue.

88

89

Site

Often, the site appropriate for the budget of a small congregation and, hence, a small church, is a plot in a suburban residential district fronting on a street, or perhaps at the corner of two streets. The congregation has the choice of being on public display or of privately enjoying its meditation. In this example the latter was preferable (**89**). The enclosing wall, constructed of ceramic cylinders with solid brick at the corners, is not found surrounding ordinary residences. The low pyramidal roof is compatible with the single-story dwellings of the neighborhood, but the building is distinctly not a dwelling. Small "birdhouse" dormer openings sprinkle the sloping roof to admit light, which, seen from inside, is like a constellation of stars. As in the preceding example, the site challenged the ingenuity of the architects.

The design of this church (**90, left**) resulted from a desire to avoid imitating the style of the old church (**right**) already standing on the property. The congregation had grown and needed more space. Three principal solutions were possible: to add to the first building, to build separately, or to move to a new location. To have added to the first would have detracted from its essential integrity. To have emulated it in a separate church would have seemed divisive. To have moved to a new site would have been unsuitable. The option to build in modern terms was therefore exercised. The architect was sensitive to the relationship between the old and new, however, and designed a church that respects the older structure while asserting its own character.

90

91a

Site

Even more than in many other instances, the shape of this church was
determined by the site chosen (**91a**). To be sure, a church could have been
built on the valley floor, but its form would have been different. The inspired
choice of this site influenced the imaginative design of the church. The
cross is a structural element as well as a symbol. The church is its own
steeple. Access to the "house built upon a rock" is gained by a winding
road behind the church, an "invisible" entrance. A glimpse through the
entrance at the rear of the church reveals the end of the access roadway
(**91b**).

91b

93

Site

For generations the "business" of the church lay in the observance of its liturgy. And so it still does. But, more recently, an added "business" is social activity, the outreach to provide service to people outside the church membership. Related to the new business, as it is to its religious mission, is the aesthetic delight of the church and its grounds. The essence of the truly modern church is its potential to inspire by its image. Gardens do more than embellish the grounds; they pay homage to nature and involve the church's spiritual role in that homage (**92, 93, 94**). Water frequently enriches the garden area, either as a natural complement to the plants or as a mirror of the church itself (**95, 96**).

94

92

95

96

97

Site

The garden of a church exterior may contribute to the aesthetics of the interior as well. At the open, spacious entrance of this church (**97**) are several boulders to guide the congregation from a broader approach to a narrower door and to remind them of the presence of nature upon entering the sanctuary.

4

INTERIORS

Plan

The arrangement, or plan, of the interior of a church varies according to the kind of service or ritual it must provide. Despite the fact that secular activities may engage much of a modern congregation's attention, the plan of a sanctuary is determined primarily by its spiritual reason for being.

The plans of many churches are rectangular, so that the congregation observes the clergy as if on a stage or screen. The religious ceremony is conveniently celebrated at one end of the rectangle, the congregation being located, sitting or standing, facing that end.

To attract attention to the liturgical area of this plan a background of rough stones sets it apart from the wooden walls of the rest of the interior, thereby drawing the eye toward it (**98**). The optical effect is increased by the succession of free-standing curved beams progressing along the nave.

98

Although the plan of this church (**99**) presupposes that its religious ceremonies will take place at the chancel, there are visual intrusions to the nave that impart to the congregation a very different kind of perception of the mission of its church than does the previous example. Whereas in the previous example attention is focused primarily on liturgical rites performed at the altar, the plan of this church includes arched side aisles that not only permit unobstrusive access to pews along the nave but also add a lateral dimension to the otherwise frontal plan. By association there results a feeling for the broadened scope of the church to include secular activities as well as religious ones. The awareness of this lateral dimension is extended by windows along the nave that reveal the everyday world without and so relate it to the world of the spirit within. The imposing succession of concrete ceiling vaults unifies the several elements of the church in a sophisticated manifestation of modern architectural aesthetics.

100

Interiors, Plan

Another scheme, or plan, to enhance the emotional impact of the liturgical area is by its dramaturgic design in which the worshipers are intimately involved. In this church (100), the circular ceiling illuminates the square-shaped seating of the celebrants below with a sense of divine blessing. It is, in fact, a halo to deify the otherwise simple architecture and, thereby, elevate the congregation into a spiritual awareness. The fact that the mundane world of city houses may be vaguely discerned through the blue glass enclosing the ark and bima (not revealed in this black and white photograph) is testimony to the reconciliation of the spirit with everyday experience.

A particular feature of the interior is the cylindrical form atop each side of the columns that flank the bima, relating them to the classic Ionic scrolls of ancient times. In fact, they articulate a transition from *tradition* to *innovation*.

The most obvious design to involve both the ministry and the congregation is the environmental concept, in which there is virtually no distinction or separation between them. This design may be square, circular, oval, or possibly an irregular shape that encourages the desired involvement (101).

In another example the altar and the pulpit are located at opposite sides of the nave to symbolize the different liturgical and secular functions of each (102).

This unusual design (103) combines the rectangular type of plan (98) and the environmental one (101). Instead of the ordinary platform to support the altar, an artist has shaped a "sculptural landscape," a mound to relate adjunct entities—altar, lectern, chair, tabernacle, and crucifix. Composed of fired clay, these were all designed and installed by the artist. Collaborating were the architects, who provided the wings for this liturgical theater. Thus, in an ingenious way, the congregation plays the roles of both audience and chorus. All seats are virtually "two on the aisle" for a communal experience.

101

102

103

104

Interiors, Plan

In each of the plans previously described the interior arrangement is understood practically at a glance. An uncommon plan, whereby the organization is gradually revealed, is to be found in the design of this church (104), which demands that the visitor explore the tortuous mystical interior for a thorough comprehension of its spiritual meaning. The architect has expressed his intentions as follows:

Just as Medieval churches were designed to enable pilgrims to circulate with ease through the church spaces, so at St. Louise a way-form or a processional path has been designed to let one be part of the totality of the abundant space of the church. The way has its beginning at the entry porch. . . . Moving eastward one enters the stone vaults of the darkened ambulatory. . . . The way flows to the Eucharistic Chapel . . . then continues to the Eucharistic tower of stone housing the Tabernacle. . . . The way moves on, as its path continues behind the choir, the Sanctuary and the Baptistry. Light enters and fades, darkness sets in, then suddenly the space, the structure, the nave and the Christocentric axis are apparent once more. The way returns to the beginning. At the beginning and the end stands the portal.

Space

Space is an extension of the plan with an important consideration: the inclusion of a third dimension that provides a "setting," a dramatic and necessary ambience for the emotional cultivation and harvest of faith. The limitless space of the roofless church (62), devoutly scraping heaven, thus connotes churchly pomp. Space, regulated by and regulating an area of worship, varies in its environmental character throughout the historical and geographical world. Diverse examples come to mind—Stonehenge, temples of the Inca, African tribal shelters in the jungle, the American Indian kiva, the trailside Zen shrine halfway up the slope of Mount Fujiyama—each adjusted to the observance of a particular religion, whether family or tribal, princely or national, or international. Space is therefore global, within the spiritual intent of a church as without. Thus the spatial dimension of the 20th-century church may be conceived appropriately in terms of its own modern mission.

Some recent church planners have inveighed against a rigid or inflexible space. Such a design, however, is not necessarily unsatisfactory, to be avoided at all costs; rather, it may be undesirable only because of the burden an exclusive design imposes on available money.

The stark simplicity of this memorial chapel (105) allows little activity other than solemn contemplation of the paintings. These are so subtle that each visitor may ponder according to the "space" within his or her own mind. The architect has placed the doorways leading into darkened passages so that they too become part of the artist's exhibition. In short, both architect and artist allow infinite scope for the imagination.

105

Although there may be monetary advantages for a multiple-use design, which must consider space along with plan, there may also be troublesome inconveniences, both for social and educational activities and for devotional purposes. Because the exercise of religious belief is the essential reason for the existence of a church, the argument for a ritually convincing space is emotionally and therefore spiritually most important. But if a given space is to serve lay programs as well, the design should ensure that the atmosphere of the sanctuary will not be impaired by psychological associations with those programs. The issue can be decided only according to the kinds of lay programs and the kind of worship concerned.

One way to reach a solution is to ask the architect to suggest an empty space consisting solely of floor, walls, and roof, which may then provide a basis for discussion with the church building committee of the congregation.

Such a space, actually constructed, is illustrated here (106). At first glance it is barren, almost uninspired. The floor of linoleum tiles, useful perhaps for social occasions, scarcely encourages a devout attitude. Covered by many chairs, however, the floor becomes unnoticed. The design of the pulpit (left foreground)—on casters, composed of curved wooden slats—conforms with the upsweeping beams. During church services the beams lead upward toward heaven, revealed by the long skylight. During social occasions they betoken the ribs of a tent, to intensify the festive environment of such events.

The organ is designed to suit either religious or secular activities. The circular arrangement of pipes corresponds to the curving beams during religious service, but calls to mind a calliope when social activities prevail. A white canopy projecting over the organ denotes its sacred function. From the distance at which the photograph was taken, the canopy, seen against the end window, forms an abstract crucifix.

107

Interiors, Space

Horizontal space, or space in depth, is often controlled by an optical illusion. The manipulation of form, texture, and light are ways by which an architect may modulate actual space to transform it into apparent space.

As may be judged by the size of the lectern at the left of the altar in this very small chapel (**107**), the end wall is literally only a few feet away. Indeed, an absolutely flat unadorned wall would seem very close. By designing a texture of pyramids in low relief illuminated by cross light from the sloping roof, however, the architect has imaginatively increased the apparent depth.

Quite differently, the actual space of this church (**108**), both laterally and vertically, is considerable. The slanting walls are blank, smooth; there is no ornament to arrest the eye, which is attracted directly to the skylight and far altar.

108 >

In striking contrast to the simplicity of surface by which space may be discerned is the use of materials to define it. Although space is essentially a void, an empty volume, it can also be experienced by observing the physical materials it contains.

An example is an altar wall (**109**), consisting of twelve huge concrete studs that form a towering fabric of measured spaces like a backdrop for the rough-hewn marble altar. A cantilevered panoply thrusts forward over the altar as a visual counterweight to the recessed space where an unadorned marble pulpit is situated. The vast configuration engages space in a compelling way that invites the eye in and out.

In a far more intimate setting (**110**) space itself, rather than objects intruding into space, commands attention. Indeed, a veritable forest of spaces encourages exploration. Replacing a conventional altar, a "picture" niche like a large empty frame, containing only a small scintillating silver cross, reflects the passing light of day as it is filtered through a blue glass panel from above. There is nothing to deter an imaginative soliloquy by the spiritual mind.

110

111

Interiors, Space

The size, or anticipated size, of a congregation obviously determines the horizontal space desired. To some extent, the number of people also influences the vertical space, or height, of a church. It is psychologically and therefore spiritually useful to have devotional "breathing" room, as in this example (111).

With the exception of some palaces and public buildings, both ancient and modern churches differ from the architectural shelters of normal domestic experience to the extent that vertical space is emotionally and spiritually exploited. As the lofty mountain lends grandeur to the landscape, so the well-designed lofty church dignifies a community. Nevertheless, both the purpose and dignity of a church may also be achieved in a more modest way if it, too, is well designed.

Vertical space is more often felt, or sensed, than scrutinized. There are occasions when the attention explores it nevertheless. In this cathedral (112) the structural texture of walls and roof, which join at the overhead crossing of colored glass, imparts an impression of splendor and invites the eye to linger.

The overhead light pouring into the otherwise dimly lit interior of the conical church (113) compels the eye to notice its sheer height.

112

113

114

Interiors, Space

In many cases the exterior shapes of churches give no indication of how the interiors have been partitioned. As with any organism, however, the inside and outside of a church should be correlated if its symbolic, functional integrity is to be convincing. The interior space will then influence certain aspects of the exterior, and vice versa.

In this instance (**114**) the fluid, irregular forms of the bima and windows are revealed on the exterior wall (**43**). The chapel is, therefore, an example of the fundamental relationship between interior and exterior to be found in all nature.

Light

Related to the concepts of plan and space is the experience of how they both look. That depends on the light by which they are observed. There is a distinction between the physical dimensions of an interior and its optical or apparent dimensions, which are subject to changes in light. As if in a theater, light dramatizes the spiritual state. The congregation responds to whatever emotional environment is thereby created.

Kind of Light

A sanctuary may be illuminated by natural or artificial light. As the latter term suggests, light may be an artifice, a scientific "trick" by which a space may be seen when the natural light of day has gone. The control and constancy of artificial light are its chief conveniences. It can be held to a uniform direction and intensity. Natural light, however, follows the cadence of the seasons, the weather, and the time of day.

Natural light welcomes nature indoors and relates worship to the external world. Artificial light draws the curtain to limit a ceremony to what lies within. Together, architect and congregation may choose one, the other, or a combination of both—for today's needs the latter choice may be the most practical.

Quality of Light

Bright light. Brilliant light, whether natural or artificial, sharpens the edges of objects as well as the textures and boundaries of areas. This results in an emphasis on the hard, matter-of-fact character of the immediate environment. It virtually eliminates the mysticism that might otherwise modify a church ceremony. If a concern for the raw realities of the everyday world is the church's mission, strong, overall light is appropriately adaptable.

115

Interiors, Light

The interior of this church (115) makes a visual statement about the metallic engineering prowess of the 20th century. The interior is sheltered from the elements, but only darkness unaided by artificial light will conceal the scintillating brilliance of the complex interior.

Similar in overall effect to the preceding example, wooden rafters supporting the roof and walls of this church (116) permit daylight to enter with the full brilliance of the outdoors, leavened only by weather conditions and the leaves of the surrounding trees.

116 ⊁

117

Interiors, Light

Subdued light. Obviously, subdued or muted light produces an effect contrary to that imposed by bright light. As with soft music, soft light encourages a passive attitude on the part of the congregation, which then tends to whisper rather than engage in noisy exchanges. Within this atmosphere the intellect can contemplate; imagination can meditate.

Light infiltrating this ingenious church (**117**) plays an important role in conveying its muted religious atmosphere. With the passage of the sun or even dim light during the hours of a cloudy day, the large window at one side of the altar produces slowly changing ''scenery.'' The rest of the church is lighted by low windows along the right-hand wall, but even they do not overpower the emotional effect of the dominant window. The rafters are observed with varying emphasis as the light changes, as is the cross, which appears and almost vanishes according to the brilliance of light upon it, symbolizing the pulsating Spirit.

Diffused light. Whether bright or subdued, light may also be diffused. There are no sharp shadows. The entire interior, somewhat indistinct perhaps, is nevertheless seen as a whole, with emphasis on no special feature.

For example, the light penetrating the wall of circular glass ''pebbles'' in this church is diffused by their varying densities (**118**). The small round openings in the brick wall absorb some of the light admitted through the wall opposite. There is no concentration of light. All the various features of the interior are equally discernible.

118

119

120

Interiors, Light

Spotlight. The spotlight is not a modern invention. A dark wall, pierced by a small opening, can admit natural light to illuminate clearly only a particular segment of the interior. A single torch can bring a mosaic to glittering life. For liturgical purposes the spotlight—natural or artificial—can be movingly effective. It focuses attention on the essential elements of celebration. It excludes ready distractions.

Light does not penetrate importantly to the area of liturgical celebration from other parts of this church (**119**). The intensity of light illuminating the celebration comes from the five circular skylights, which admit natural daylight. When that has dwindled, artificial light from the same central sources replaces it. The several spotlights may therefore be regulated at will.

In the church (**120**), the architect has sensitively employed a natural spotlight beamed from a central source above. When necessary, artificial light may also supplement the light of day. The "woodland" of beams recalls a forest glade, where firelight was the source of illumination for tribal ceremonies in primitive cultures. The design is thus a reiteration in modern terms of longstanding spiritual imagery.

Arts

A church, designed and constructed with mindful attention to the wishes and approval of a congregation, might seem to be complete. However, there are symbolic overtones, ornaments, that can enrich the essential mission of a given church and that need to be added in order to advance its stature from the prosaic to the poetic.

Ornament is, possibly, too simple a word to describe the importance to a church of such elements as sculpture, painting, windows, fabrics, and the like—all of which contribute grace and beauty to the interior. But they also combine to advocate the meaning of the church itself.

Briefly, so varied are the many symbolic embellishments, available or to be commissioned, that it is impossible to stipulate what article should be appropriate except by examining the possibilities for a given church. The essence of a new church, as with its contents, is to refresh and stimulate a congregation that seeks to revitalize itself, or to become a new, adventuresome, and devout body. The style of the furnishings must be visually appropriate to the style of the interior design. Both should enhance the tenets of the particular church.

Furnishings

Upon entering a church the eye is prone to sum up its mission immediately. Not only do the plan, space, and light describe that mission, but the design of furniture—altar, organ, pews, font, communion railing, and the like—also distinguishes its character. Spiritual insight and a corresponding imaginative design are to be sought by a church planning committee in order to achieve a sympathetic correlation between the architecture and the furnishings that are an integral part of it. Because the sanctuary is what might be called the reward of the architect, the architect may be requested to advise on, or indeed to prescribe the style of furnishings to be incorporated within the design.

Fonts. Several faiths originated in arid lands where an oasis meant the revitalization of physical existence and, hence, of spiritual life. Water became not only a practical element for survival but also a symbolic agent of redemption from parched suffering. In contrast to our modern scientific knowledge of the deep, water represented the mystical unknown from which one emerged cleansed for renewed life. Because this religious heritage has survived until this day, receptacles are installed in the church to offer therapeutic spiritual benefits.

The designs of these fonts differ according to the circumstances of each congregation, but also in accordance with the aesthetic sensitivity of the architect involved.

As has been suggested, the rite of baptism (from an ancient Greek word meaning "to dip") is profound. Therefore, total submersion in the transcendent element of water and ascension from it (or merely symbolic sprinkling) is a ceremony for which members of a church program committee, together with its chosen architect, must design a facility to satisfy their own expression of its religious significance.

121

In this example (**121**), in full view of the assembled congregation, those who are to be baptized are admitted through·a door in a bronze sculptural screen down steps into the depth of a concrete pool lined with tiles. The abstract relief on the screen is intended to symbolize the inspired essence of heaven as reflected in the rippling baptismal water below. That the design was produced by controlling high explosives is intriguing, but it has little relevance for the baptismal ritual, except possibly to propose an affinity between technical and spiritual fundamentals.

122

Arts, Fonts

In certain instances baptism is considered to be a personal ceremony to be witnessed by a few rather than by an entire congregation. For this purpose it is possible to set aside a special chapel, or baptistry. This is particularly important in those instances where a church wishes to provide ecumenical services, for the baptistry can then be designed in a general way without inconvenience to other functions of the church. This sunken pebble-lined basin is a case in point (122). The abstract mobile sculpture suspended above the font creates ripples in the air to echo those in the water and add to the inspiration of the environment.

At the entrance of this interior (123) one comes upon a quadrilateral font that draws attention from the otherwise attractive features vying for equal recognition: the brickwork, its structure, the ceiling, the lighting, etc. The position of the font, opposite the entrance at the rear of the nave, is an architectural statement of its significance. Its geometrical yet sculptural design supports that prominence.

123 >

124

125

126

Arts, Fonts

In this instance (**124**) access to the font is gained from the corridor upon entering or leaving the sanctuary. An added feature, however, is the opportunity its location provides for members of the congregation to participate in a baptismal ceremony without leaving their seats, nor intruding on its relative privacy.

An alternative location for a font, rather than close to the sanctuary entrance, is within the immediate reach of the chancel. In such a position it draws attention to its purpose along with those separate purposes of the altar, organ, choir, and other accouterments of a church service.

The water-worn boulder from a local glacial moraine (**125**) adds something more to the symbolic meaning of the area than would a conventional baptismal vessel. The natural hollow found in the stone relates the essence of nature to the human imagination that finds divine meaning in it.

It might not be too far amiss to assert that a garden landscape within a church is superior to two gardens outside;. an especially strong case might be made in this instance (**126**), wherein the amphitheater confronts a resplendent garden chancel. Baptismal water is part of the terrace design.

127

Arts, Organs

Organs. The emotional contribution of music to church liturgy is as inspiring as space and light. It is a unifying experience joining clergy with congregation. The visual evidence of music in a church is the rhythmic design of organ pipes, which often are but mute emblems rather than producers of sound. The true pipes are frequently located in modest positions out of view. Nevertheless, the decorative eloquence of "pipery" is a distinctive addition to the symbolic interior of church architecture.

The several segments of this complex organ (**127**) are situated on platforms, or balconies, much as differing instruments of a symphony orchestra might be disposed. They are designed to be seen as well as be heard, as the members of the orchestra are meant to be both seen and heard. The wooden strips on the wall at right and the vertical louvres over the window at left are designed to conform to the stacked pattern of the pipes. The many elements of a church interior should possess such relevancies if the church is to present a coordinated image.

The heavenward sweep of the beams that support the conical roof of this church (**128**) determine the appropriate design of organ pipes as a musical accompaniment to those shapes. The interior garden contributes harmoniously to the emotional influence of the total interior.

Similarly, a canopy of draped wooden slats, which filters light into this interior (**129**), provides the motif for the design of pipes rising as a melodic counterpoint to the conformation of the suspended ceiling.

128

129

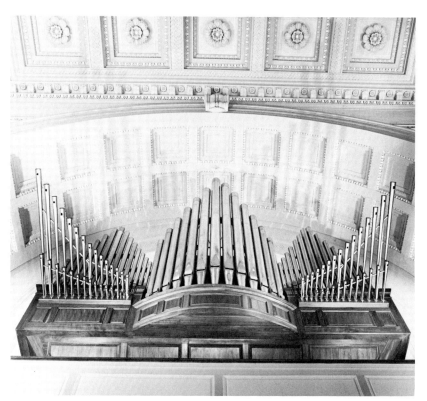

130

Arts, Organs

For centuries trumpets provided the stentorian voices associated with religious ceremonies as well as with royal pageantry. The organ pipes of these two examples (**130, 131**) both project horizontally in the regal manner of trumpets once held by brawny musicians.

In the first (**130**), "sixty-one gold pipes are especially commanding as they form the heroic *trompette-en-chamade*" (literally, to sound a call for peace from on high).

In the second (**131**), the horizontal pipes hail the presence of Christ in Majesty, whose figure, cloaked in gold leaf, rises radiantly above them.

131 >

133

Arts, Organs

Organ pipes need not be ranked in linear order like troops on parade. Architects, and congregations, are at liberty to seek the design of an organ that may best suit the aesthetics of the church, both acoustical and visual. Two quite different examples are worth noting.

One is an organ music box in concept (**132**). The pipes are arranged, appropriately, to harmonize with the structure of the ceiling, as well as with the grid of platforms and pews on the floor below. Placed in a prominent alcove, the organ box is an abstract sculpture set on a pedestal. Considered in another way, but probably not the intention of the architect, it becomes a masque (squint to discover eyes, nose, and open mouth) to give voice on behalf of the liturgy conducted at the altar elsewhere in the church.

In a second example (**133**) the design of pipes virtually determines the aesthetics of the interior. Occupying a central position in a spectacular church (**66**), the rhythmic formation of these organ pipes is akin to a sacred ballet dramatizing the rest of the sanctuary.

< **132**

134

Sculpture

Sculpture can contribute to the emotional atmosphere of a church. If its images are literal illustrations of special religious themes, the mind of the observer becomes focused on those themes. The freedom of imagination is then limited. If the work is more abstract it encourages contemplation and thereby enriches the religious experience. The particular design of an interior will often suggest to an artist an appropriate style or image. Similarly, a work that has previously been independently created should be selected with regard to the interior so that the art and architecture may complement each other.

For centuries, sculpture has both embellished and given literary substance to all sorts of architecture. Sculpture provides a commentary that the functional design of a building can imply but cannot readily define. Even so, sculpture, like painting, loses its inspirational value if it is too explicit in context. An architectural committee, determined to contrive the widest emotional scope for the needs of its members, should provide a setting that will stimulate and satisfy those needs. Sculpture, along with painting, can contribute much in a variety of ways.

In one exalted instance, sculpture is afforded shelter that the congregation is not (134). The holy dove draws up the enfolding robes of the Virgin, whose semiabstract image is protected by a sheltering canopy while the congregation humbly stands without (62). People do not so much participate in as witness the sculptured event. In this context the sculpture is significantly personalized.

By contrast, the sculpture screen (135) is an essay illustrating biblical events, which invites the congregation to participate in the liturgical message conveyed.

135 >

133

Yet another instance of the power of sculpture to communicate spiritual qualities is the golem (**136**). A religious robot that first appears in medieval Jewish folklore, a golem is endowed with magical life but contrived by human ingenuity. In that respect it supplies moral support to resist oppression. As sculpture, the piece is close to the folk art in which it is rooted. As a modern concept it is both traditional and innovative.

Close to and yet far from folk legend is the Christian account of the crucifixion. In many cases, its representation has become overly sentimental because years of veneration have persuaded followers to seek redemption by adoration. Regarded callously, however, it was a brutal event, as are all acts of violence and torture. This agonized, distorted figure (**137**) is a humane, powerful protest against suffering, rather than a penitent representation of it.

When considering the universal need for a religious conviction that will provide truly spiritual support, it seems appalling that there have been and still are "holy wars," meaningless violence, among those who choose different methods to express their concepts of divinity.

A passionate plea for reconciliation is, perhaps subconsciously, expressed through the emotions of one artist who has envisaged figures to symbolize similar feelings experienced by two avowedly different faiths.

In a Jewish temple Moses, with arms and voice upraised, reveals the majesty of God to the people (**138**). In a Catholic sanctuary the supplicant Christ in Glory (**139**) is conceived by the same artist, in somewhat the same posture, as the divine mediator to reach the congregation on behalf of "the Lord." Each differs according to the two faiths, yet the affinity of the dual ecstasies is explicit.

136

137

138

139

140

141

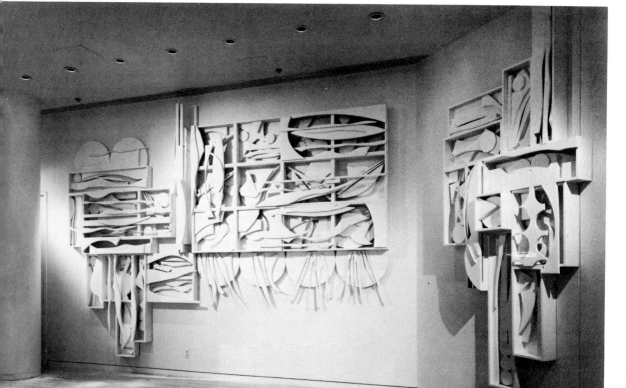

142

Arts, Sculpture

In certain cultures, past and present, the arts have best represented philosophical concepts by abstract means. It was not possible to explain basic issues by representing everyday people or events. In modern years many new concepts have evolved, which likewise can only be described in abstract ways. Several examples may serve as illustrations.

The Flood (**140**) is a bas-relief that describes a cataclysm, an act of nature, which is intimately associated with biblical legend as well as immediate human experience. An overwhelming sense of flowing and inundation is the motif of the sculptor.

Also modulated in abstract terms is the theme of the twelve apostles, which is constructed on the chapel walls of St. Peter's Church (Lutheran), New York City, so that the confined interior becomes an imaginative refuge for those who come to meditate (**141**).

Moreover, sculpture may occasionally describe holy attributes, as in the mystical rays of metallic spines that bestow a visual blessing above the altar of the Portsmouth Priory in Rhode Island (**142**) or in the shower of "angelic flakes" that serves to filter the light pouring through the oculus, the "eye toward heaven," of the profoundly moving chapel at the Massachusetts Institute of Technology (**143**).

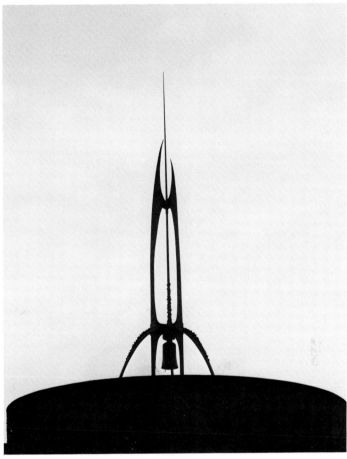

144

Arts, Sculpture

The latter structure is surmounted by a studiously conceived belfry (**144**) to affirm, by a graceful design of mathematical curves, the pertinence of art to science.

As with architecture, the essence of sculpture is form defined through materials and spaces. Architecture and sculpture are also akin in that both exhibit an emotional, indeed devout, sense of purpose when they are imaginatively expressed.

< 143

One sculptural example is a metallic shaft pinpointed upon a tetrahedron (**145**). Despite the title, *Broken Obèlisk,* it suggests a dialogue between the base, which is a symbol of permanence or eternity, and the tenuously balanced shaft implying impermanence and so symbolizing the delicate existence of transitory life. Arising from the fugitive reflections of a shallow pool, it is a positive introduction to the philosophically abstract painting in the adjacent memorial chapel (**105**).

In a sense, an interior may be its own architectural sculpture. There are instances, moreover, when the architect turns sculptor, as it were, to add symbolic meaning to the design.

The arching shapes of these beams and the intervals between them (**146**), for example, are sculpturesque in character while forming a frame for the altar and the wall behind it. The wall is given symbolic meaning by the pattern of the brickwork, which resembles a crucifix, a sculptural pattern.

145

146

Sculpture outdoors also possesses liturgical significance. A garden may not only contribute to the aesthetic presence of a church but—much as do windows, paintings, or statuary—may also inform and remind the congregation of a holy event. This small church (**147**) has been built in a wooded lot where most of the trees have been spared; they cover the church with the tranquility of nature. Incorporated in the tiny court leading to the entrance of the church is a *Garden of Gethsemane*. Shrubs, flowers, and the architecture of the church combine to form an "elegaic theater" wherein the bronze figures of Christ in agony and his sleeping disciples are set. Those who pass cannot help but enter the church with compassion and humility.

The architect of the small meditation room of the United Nations (**148**) preferred to avoid symbolic reference to any particular faith, yet he felt the need for something sculptural to enrich an otherwise empty space. He selected, for that purpose, a block of iron ore scaled to the dimensions of the space. Its intrinsic meaning may, perhaps, be discovered in its universal simplicity: a matrix of the earth smelted and shaped by human mastery.

The geometric forms of the painting enliven what might otherwise be overly monotonous space. It is significant that Dag Hammarskjold, Secretary General of the United Nations, took particular interest in the design of the chapel. With his personal encouragement, all—sculpture, painting, and architecture—have been united to produce an inspired serenity.

147

148

Textiles

Textiles may contribute to the image of a church no less impressively than other furnishings. An example is this resplendent ark covered with a hand-tufted tapestry which elevates a material human skill to seraphic ardor (**149**).

Windows and Paintings

Windows are important aesthetic elements in the design of a church and should be conceived as part of its total image, for they importantly influence the mood of the interior. Whether the purpose of installing windows is to regulate light, admit air, provide a spiritual connection with nature outside, serve as symbols through the medium of colored glass, or a combination of these, depends on how the congregation views its role internally and in its community.

Windows are almost always designed for the particular church where they are to be installed. That is rarely true of paintings, which are commonly composed independently of special locations, yet are not without spiritual content, whether consciously or subconsciously devised. Naturally an artist is happy to receive a commission that will help intensify his or her inspiration.

Windows. A window can contribute to the internal quality of a church by the visual emotions it provokes and by the lucid meanings it imparts. Because the "personality" of a church is unique, its demands on the inspiration of an artist are akin to its dependence on the imagination of an architect. The church benefits from the particular attention of both. No commonplace formula can suffice.

An example is the commission that motivated the design of this resplendent wall, which may only by analogy be called a window (**150**).

149 >

150

Arts, Windows and
Paintings

In a series of notes on his work the artist wrote that for his motif he
selected the text from Genesis 1:1-4, KJV:

*In the beginning God created the heaven and the earth. And the earth was
without form, and void; and darkness was upon the face of the deep. And
the Spirit of God moved upon the face of the waters. And God said, Let
there be light: and there was light. And God saw the light, that it was good:
and God divided the light from the darkness.*

The artist continues, *"I now made it my desire to try to interpret this biblical
text and to reveal, if only to a small degree, the meaning and beauty in the
idea of the work and act of God; to convey the strange forces in which we
are integrated and in which our destiny is involved."*

A church window need not "tell a story" or communicate recognizable
symbols to be spiritually effective. Moreover, abstract art is not foreign to
religious experience, as the glorious rose windows of Gothic churches
remind us.

In a similar vein the artist who composed this window (**151**) employed the
freedom of abstraction to unify the outer and inner spirit by metaphorically
refining raw external light to the revelational internal perception of it. In such
terms the window penetrates to a more profound level than mere scriptural
elucidation. Inherent in it is the confrontation of worldly corrosion with godly
splendor, of profaneness with redemption.

151

152a

Arts, Windows and Paintings

Occasionally, an architect may advise a church building committee that a combination of abstract and symbolic images may be appropriate, as in these examples (**152a, 152b**). The architect has expressed that relationship briefly:

For the sake of color relationships, only seen directly in the glass and projected on to the deep window reveals, I elected to have the glass patterns in abstract geometry, non-representational. The only exception is the insertion of the little sailboat of St. Jude in which he was said to have travelled the Mediterranean sea on his Christian missions.

It seems obvious that the selection of an architect involves considering not only the architect's aesthetic regard for the design of the structure but also his or her sensitivity toward the particular ritual symbolism concerned. For example, the architect (in the instance cited) needed to know that St. Jude was the apostle, brother of James, the fisherman, and must have been well acquainted with the art of sailing. Therefore the symbol of the boat is apt. The overall meaning is broader, however, for a ship was also a frequent symbol of the Church (whence the architectural term *nave*) to buoy life upon troubled waters toward the harbor of heavenly salvation.

152b

153

Arts, Windows and
Paintings

For centuries in the history of Christian building biblical images provided
dazzling embellishments for churches. They were not windows in the early
years, but mosaic panels executed and embedded in the masonry with
exquisite craftsmanship. As newer architectural technology permitted larger
window space to be constructed, the splendor of Gothic colored glass
appeared. Although these bejeweled windows excluded a view to the
outdoors, they admitted light as a means of enriching the religious figures
indoors.

In contrast, these two painted glass panels (153) welcome the spiritual eye
outward. The colored illusion of living wind-blown leaves attracts attention to
the natural landscape beyond as a symbol to relate the devout aspirations of
the interior to their divine source.

Normally, a symbol is a visual shorthand to express an accepted concept.
Occasionally, symbols are invented to paraphrase a special circumstance
but, because they are unfamiliar, their meanings may be unclear. At such
times words can hint at the aesthetic functions of the symbols.

154

To interpret the symbolism of the handsomely bizarre chapel (**43, 114**) the architect himself has come to the rescue. It is important to keep in mind, however, that his words would have little power without illustrations of the symbolic forms he invented: *"The overriding concern, architecturally, was the integration of art and architecture."* He also stresses his feeling for the integration of architecture and nature by describing the two large copper chandeliers as depicting natural floral forms. The architect has elaborated elsewhere (**154**) on his feeling for a harmonious blend of art, architecture, nature, and religion:

In a religious sense, I tried to incorporate biblical influences in the architecture to express the Jewish faith and its aspirations. . . . For example, the Ark is a sky-lighted dome, which has a strong shaft of light, using the sun to symbolize nature and God as a continuing presence in the world. . . . The general concept of the stained glass was the biblical story of Jacob's dream, where the bones of the children of Israel were scattered throughout the desert and God said he would bring them back to life. In this case, the shapes of the chapel are reminiscent of the bones of the Children of Israel and the stained glass, with God's light, gives them the spark of life.

156

Arts, Windows and
Paintings

The artist Ben Shahn was a compassionate painter, especially during the agonizing decade of the economic depression (1930–1940). He was always devoted to the humble throngs of people and advocated their ennoblement with fresh symbols.

An example is illustrated by Temple Beth Zion, Buffalo, New York (**155**). The commanding window represents, according to the artist, *"the massive upturned hand, symbolizing* creation. *Lines, swirling about the hand, represent the voice out of the whirlwind that spoke to the suffering Job."*

Flanking the window are columns into which have been set Venetian glass tesserae to recall the instruction of the ten commandments. The symbolic integration of architecture and the design of its details is both traditional and innovative.

Painting. In the past, religious painting usually depicted people or particular events. Today, it is apt to be illustrative of philosophical or theological concepts and is necessarily abstract because the concepts themselves are abstract.

An example is this painting (**156**). The artist attributes the inspiration for it to an address given at Boston University by Howard Thurman, who referred to *"spears of sorrow becoming shafts of light."* In a painterly response the artist notes: *The painting moves from dark and painful colors on the left, through an area of nature, forms and colors of growing things, to a large iris-like sprouting leaf form on the right, symbolic of the energy of renewed growth and the flower to come from it.*

The painting was the center of a service on the occasion of its dedication as an addition to a church collection. It is an instance of how a congregation can bring modern cultural insights into the being of its church.

< 155

157

Arts, Windows and Paintings

Paradoxically, an artist's intent *need* never be questioned, but *should* always be. The paradox can be resolved by noting, in the first place, that the inspiration of the work of art originates with the artist. In the second place, a work of art that purports to communicate may do so only by questions that relate the experience of the viewer to that of the artist. Unless such a sharing of experience can be established, communication and meaning cannot be transmitted.

In a narrative account of the *Jesse Ensign* (**157**) the artist fulfills her abstract independence and thereby anticipates the question as to its meaning.

A strong influence was the Jesse *window in Chartres cathedral, France.... A rough description of the imagery shows Jesse lying on the ground and from his pelvis a tree has taken root.... My painting describes an emblem, or sign, instead of a tree. Surrounding the emblem are eight medallions. The* bottom medallion has the mark of the Christogram, the other seven have the names of those listed in the genealogy of Abraham to Jesus.

A church can appropriately seek or commission such paintings to enrich its environment.

Explication is not always the way to understand abstract art. The abstract image should tell its own story. Nevertheless, when an artist is willing to do so, he or she can give a verbal description that may illuminate what the image cannot always do for popular comprehension.

To a discerning eye, the figure of Christ on the cross is evident in this painting (158). The artist's comment may help those who do not immediately see it to search further.

My paintings of the crucifixion usually present a hopeful Christ, but sometimes my painting is of a resigned Christ and, frequently, of a defiant Christ. Only the arms, hands, head and cross are shown. . . . I am interested in the livingness of the ideas inherent in the crucifixion rather than simply in the factual story of the actual event.

158

159

Arts, Windows and
Paintings

Even more abstract than the preceding painting, which is contemplated
objectively, is this philosophical painting, which enfolds the viewer both
physically and subjectively (**159**). Rather than attempt to interpret the
experience, it is best to let the artist translate it from his own visual
language to his verbal one:

*The sense of tragedy in the sixties and seventies insisted itself upon me as
the subject matter for the walls I had been asked to paint in the Neuberger
Museum (State University, Purchase, N.Y.). . . . In this heroic space . . .the
vertical forms are symbols which conform to my understanding of reality—
the inseparability of life from death, the reconciliation of opposites. . . . I
have hoped that students . . . whose minds are crammed with imposed
knowledge, could enter this room and possess themselves of their own
thoughts, could react to the paintings as an environment for meditation. . . .
In such a meditative context, I thought of the room as a cathedral: the
central axis as the nave, the two doors as transepts, the black wall as the
West wall . . . and the red wall as the apse—the source of light and hope.*

Obviously, the fact that the painting is not materially incorporated in an
existing church in no way detracts from its religious intent. A church setting
might possibly make that intent more explicit. In turn, planning for such
paintings for new churches, as noted earlier, can enhance the church's
spiritual reason for being.

Part III   Renovation

Destruction of churches by fire, wind, water, or whatever cause produces benumbing anguish. Usually the contents are lost as well as the building. Indeed, it is fortunate if people do not perish in the process. The most painful stress occurs during the aftermath, when a decision must be made as to what action to take: Should the congregation disband? Should it be merged with another, if one is to be found, and if so are the two compatible? Should the destroyed structure be carefully restored? Should a new design be adopted as a symbol for the future, whether upon the same or a new site? Where will the needed money come from? From a practical point of view, the last question may seem to be the most important at first. Answers to the others, however, will provide the best insight to the future mission of the church. There is no pat solution. That must be determined by the congregation itself.

160a

Renovation

There are times when the historical and artistic qualities of a church are such that to restore it as faithfully as possible is more felicitous than to build in a different fashion or to disband the congregation.

An unusually heavy snowfall collapsed the central section of this admirable Greek Revival structure (**160a**) some three quarters of a century after it had been built. The Swedenborgian congregation believed that nothing could reaffirm the devout intent of the founders as well as building anew in the original image, even though times and styles had changed considerably.

Both ends of the church had been left standing by the storm; it was not too speculative a task to reconstruct it, with minor alterations as reinforcement against future disaster (**160b**). There had been no steeple. Thus, the basic Greek temple form was faithfully reproduced without excessive expense.

161

Renovation

In the historical context of Boston, Massachusetts, the congregation of this church (**161**), which had been gutted by fire, decided that some physical evidence of the many years of the building's existence, viewed as a spiritual community, should remain to be revered by future members. The congregation also felt that anything to be built on the burned site should be as simple as possible, for both financial and aesthetic considerations. Nothing new should detract from or compete with the old steeple rising with fresh witness from its ashes.

A typical New England church, dignified by an elegant steeple—the kind of image so many congregations across the country associate with the idea of a church—was totally destroyed by fire. Its spacious interior had been adorned with a miscellany of architectural details borrowed from classical and Renaissance styles. It was a proper example of mid-19th century taste and a benevolent inheritance for those who worshiped there even a hundred years later. Its loss was literally irreparable and so it was decided, over the strong objections of some, to build anew in the modern manner, for nothing remained to be historically treasured. The architectural eloquence of the old interior (**162a**) had been imparted by the ornament applied to the surfaces of what would otherwise have been bleak walls. In the new, flexible interior (**162b**) the sculpture-like interlocking spaces become their own distinguished ornament.

162a

162b

163a

Renovation

In a somewhat similar instance, fire destroyed this low wooden church (**163a**) beyond reasonable repair. This misfortune was not so poignant, however, because there were no historic remains to preserve, nor any argument for rebuilding it as it had been. The congregation decided to raise the money to build a new, more substantial structure (**163b**). A brick-paved open court and some planting lend distinction to the otherwise austere stone facade. The long ramp to aid the handicapped is not only a practical extension of the entrance but also guides the ablebodied as well as the handicapped into the body of the church.

163b

164a

164b

The scale of a new church building normally depends on three factors: the size of the congregation, its projected growth, and the money available. Not uncommonly, the growth proves to be more rapid than anticipated. It then becomes necessary to seek additional facilities. These may consist of new space attached to the old, or a wholly new structure. Whether the old building is retained or abandoned depends on local circumstances.

Rather than spoil the unity of this existing church (**164a**), built in the 13th-century English style, the congregation chose to expand physically by constructing a separate church (**164b**). The old one was to remain as an adjunct chapel. Outwardly, the two are visually united by similar stonework, but the forms of each, though complementary, are different. The architect of the new building was instructed to *"build with boldness and imagination in the media and materials of our time"* in order that the new church might *"speak with relevance to the age in which we live."*

165

Renovation

To be sure, there are times when the existing building has little architectural merit. In such cases there may be aesthetic reasons for adopting a new image as well as convenience in attaching it to the old.

Here (165), the link is a corridor between the old convent and the new chapel. Above the corridor is a "leaning tower" containing bells to sound the joining of old and new.

Sometimes a church's need for additional space is more modest than what would be provided by a new structure. Existing property can then be skillfully and appropriately converted.

An example is this secular wing of a Gothic-style church (166a), which contained offices and meeting and utility rooms that were no longer used. The architect was bound to adhere to the overall exterior shape of the wing but was at liberty to reorganize it in other respects, both inside and out, as his judgment, together with that of the church committee, saw fit. This resulted in an entrance and paved court giving new access to the wing (166b). The corridor between the wing and the church was modified by changing the Gothic arch above the small entrance to a medieval-style architrave and replacing the nondescript window above it with a small Gothic outline.

166a

166b

166c

Renovation

In contrast to the Gothic ornament of the adjacent church, the new facade is bare, but the white accents over the new doorways emphasize a deference to the adjacent older style. In the interior (**166c**) there is no trace of the former offices. The open space, the severe, unadorned walls, the irregular rhythm of the windows, the bare slate floor and wooden ceiling, the movable rush chairs, and the concealed artificial lights are, all together, the signs of the times—these times.

Space for this small chapel was "discovered" in the cluttered basement storage (**167a**) of the existing large chapel, or church, which was constructed to house the compulsory church attendance of some eight hundred to a thousand students. Although that service had been nondenominational, the atmosphere had not satisfied the ritual needs of the Roman Catholic or Jewish participants. The new basement worship area was designed, without windows, as flexible space for the use of any faith (**167b**). Artists were commissioned to provide movable ceremonial objects appropriate to the celebration of each faith. Illustrated are the ark and menorah designed and fabricated for Jewish services by a school art instructor, G. Shertzer.

With the abolition of required attendance the use of the large church decreased, whereas the demand for the small one increased beyond all expectations. Although seemingly fragmented, the nondenominational congregation retained its ecumenical function.

167a

167b

Part IV   Beyond the Church

Manifestations of human piety are immeasurable. There are archaeological evidences of it in the remote domains of prehistory and demonstrations of its influence on social behavior since then to the present time. The quantity of religious structures in the United States alone, from which these examples of architectural design have been drawn, betokens the pervasive nature of this piety. Beyond religious structures, there are further examples of its presence. Church builders concerned with the effect of aesthetics on people's spiritual emotions might well take account of such examples.

168

In times past, the church or temple was usually the focus or center of community life, both sacred and profane. Unable to assume such authority, the modern congregation most commonly reaches into the community in an effort to bring it within its fold. Consequently, architects planning sanctuaries suitable for today are frequently asked to design additional space where the church may exercise its broad social functions. Indeed, most of the churches illustrated in this book possess such facilities, which are essentially beyond the church's liturgical existence.

An example is this seminar or meeting room for small groups of people (168). The rectilinear shapes of the movable furniture are in keeping with the cubical space of the room itself, no matter how the individual pieces are placed. Despite the severity of the geometric design, or perhaps because of it, maximum flexibility is achieved. The cruciform shape of the abstract painting reinforces the similar shape of the wall upon which it is located. Thus, although the room serves secular activities, it emanates the spiritual essence of the church to which it is joined.

169

Temporary quarters, for whatever reason they are needed, have little to do with architecture. Occasionally, however, a special religious event takes place involving such numbers of people that no existing shelter can accommodate them. Years ago, religious processions and pageantry were commonplace, often proceeding from the marketplace or city square to the church.

On the occasion of the visit of Pope John Paul II to Boston in 1979, a suitable pavilion was constructed—an outdoor sanctuary—to honor his presence (169). It was without walls so that all might see and take part. The structure consisted of transparent planes, individually supported, as are the separate religions of the world, yet portraying a unity symbolizing the inward spirit of the human race. It was temporary by some standards, but it was permanent for the duration of the visit.

170a

Beyond the Church

For those who are observant there are a variety of religious experiences outside the church. Among them is a memorial to six million Jews murdered in Nazi Germany. In an Atlanta, Georgia, cemetery rough-hewn stones have been assembled to compose a shrine that can be contemplated simultaneously from both within and without its walls (**170a**). There is no roof, for none is needed. The bare simplicity is in itself impressive. The monument is an example of the organic relationship of outside and inside.

Upon entering the small labyrinth (**170b**) visitors come upon six metal torches identifying ashes gathered from the Nazi holocaust. A tablet reads: *"The voice of thy brother's blood cries unto me from the ground."* And elsewhere, *"For these I weep."* The visitor's departure is solemn.

170b >

171

Beyond the Church

Not all structures that predicate a divinity are churches. This stone landscape (**171**) evolved from the labor of one man who cut, pieced, and placed blocks from an abandoned quarry, making of them a sculptured garden. He literally recreated nature in its own image. Whether he was motivated religiously or not is of little consequence; although it was not intended as a shrine, the aesthetic conviction of this monument provides more spiritual inspiration than many a banal church.

Human beings tend to find faith in themselves through faith in nature. Nature, being a divine manifestation, provides a lesson for those planning a church by showing that majesty (**172**) and delicacy (**173**) are akin. The reverent manipulation of nature by people, as well as the enterprises—large or small—of nature itself, signify the presence of the Spirit. A church should be the covenant of both.

172

173

List of Illustrations

66 North Christian Church, Columbus, IN. Architect: Eero Saarinen and Associates. Photographer: Balthazar Korab.

67 Portsmouth Priory, Roman Catholic, Portsmouth, RI. Architect: Belluschi, Anderson, Beckwith and Haible. Photographer: Joseph W. Molitor.

68 St. Peter's Roman Catholic Church, Manset, Mt. Desert, ME. Architect: Willoughby Marshall. Photographer: Robert Danora.

69 Church of St. James the Fisherman, Episcopal, Wellfleet, MA. Architect: Olav Hammarström. Photographer: © Ezra Stoller.

70 Church of St. Peter Claver, Roman Catholic, West Hartford, CT. Architect: Russell Gibson von Dohlen. Photographer: Charles N. Pratt.

71 Congregation Or Veshalom, Atlanta, GA. Architect: Benjamin Hirsch.

72 Altamonte Springs Chapel, Altamonte Springs, FL. Architect: Nils Schweizer and Associates. Photographer: William F. Grover.

73 Covenant Presbyterian Church, Albany, GA. Architect: Belluschi and Brannen. Photographer: IFRAA Collection.

74 St. Mary's Cathedral, Roman Catholic, San Francisco, CA. Architect: McSweeney, Ryan and Lee. Design Consultants: Belluschi and Nervi. Photographer: Morley Baer.

75 Second Congregational Society, Unitarian, Concord, NH. Architect: Hugh Stubbins and Associates. Photographer: Maris-Stoller Associates.

76 St. David's Episcopal Church, Wilmington, DE. Architect: Harold Wagoner and Associates. Photographer: IFRAA Collection.

77 First Presbyterian Church, Hayward, CA. Architect: Culver Heaton. Photographer: IFRAA Collection.

78 Wayfarer's Chapel, Church of the New Jerusalem, Swedenborgian, Palos Verdes, CA. Architect: Lloyd Wright. Photographer: IFRAA Collection.

79a First Presbyterian Church, Stamford, CT. Architect: Wallace Harrison. Photographer: © Cunningham-Werdnigg.

79b First Presbyterian Church, The Maguire Memorial Carillon Tower, Stamford, CT. Architect: Wallace Harrison. Photographer: © Cunningham-Werdnigg.

80 Chapel and Monastery for the Basilian Fathers of Mariapoch, Byzantine Rite, Catholic, Matawan, NJ. Architect: Witfield and Remick.

81 Third Church of Christ Scientist, Washington DC. Architect: I.M. Pei and Partners. Design Consultant: Araldo Cossuta. Photographer: Gorchev and Gorchev.

82 St. Jude Roman Catholic Church, North Grand Rapids, MI. Architect: Progressive Design Associates. Photographer: Balthazar Korab.

83 Abbey Church, St. John's University, Roman Catholic, Collegeville, MN. Architect: Marcel Breuer, Hamilton P. Smith and Associates. Photographer: Hedrich Blessing.

84 Gethsemane Lutheran Church, Virginia, MN. Architect: Jyring and Whiteman and Associates. Photographer: IFRAA Collection.

85 Hillside Church, Interfaith, Rose Hill, CA. Architect: Albert C. Martin and Associates. Photographer: IFRAA Collection.

86 Pacific Beach Congregational Church, Pacific Beach, CA. Architect: Richard John Lareau and Associates. Photographer: George Lyons.

87a St. Peter's Lutheran Church, New York, NY. Architect: Hugh Stubbins and Associates. Photographer: Norman McGrath.

87b St. Peter's Lutheran Church, looking down to exterior, New York, NY. Architect: Hugh Stubbins and Associates. Photographer: Copyright Ezra Stoller.

88 Civic Center Synagogue, New York, NY. Architect: William N. Breger. Photographer: Robert Galbraith.

89 Elysian Fields Methodist Church, New Orleans, LA. Architect: George A. Saunders and Associates. Photographer: IFRAA Collection.

90 Christ Church, Episcopal, Concord, MA. Architect: John H. Chapman, Harry B. Little, and Frank Owen—new church, Pietro Belluschi. Photographer: Alice Moulton.

91a Chapel of the Holy Cross, Roman Catholic, Sedona, AZ. Architect: Anshen and Allen. Photographer: Julius Shulman.

91b Chapel of the Holy Cross, Roman Catholic, interior looking toward entrance driveway, Sedona, AZ. Architect: Anshen and Allen. Photographer: Julius Shulman.

92 St. Mary's Convent, Roman Catholic, Tucson, AZ. Architect: Anderson, De Bartolo, and Pan.

93 Covenant Presbyterian Church, Albany, GA. Architect: Belluschi and Brannen.

94 St. John's, Episcopal, Midland, MI. Architect: Alden Dow. Photographer: Gerald Gard.

95 Miramar Chapel, Interfaith, La Jolla, CA. Architect: Richard J. Neutra and Robert Alexander. Photographer: Julius Shulman.

96 St. John's Episcopal Church, Midland, MI. Architect: Alden Dow. Photographer: IFRAA Collection.

97 Unitarian Church, Norwalk, CT. Architect: Victor Lundy. Photographer: IFRAA Collection.

98 St. Paul's Episcopal Church, Mt. Vernon, WA. Architect: Durham, Anderson and Freed.

99 St. Mark's Lutheran Church, Norwich, CT. Architect: John MacL. Johansen. Photographer: Robert Stahman.

100 Ramaz School Chapel, Orthodox Jewish, New York, NY. Architect: Conklin and Rossant. Photographer: Wolfgang Hoyt-Esto.

101 All Souls Unitarian Church, Schenectady, NY. Architect: Edward Durrell Stone. Photographer: Ken Staley.

102 Our Lady of Hope, Roman Catholic, Baltimore, MD. Architect: Gaudreau. Photographer: M.E. Warren.

103 Newman Center Chapel, Roman Catholic, University of California, Berkeley, CA. Artist: Stephen DeStaebler. Architect: Mario Campi. Photographer: Karl H. Riek.

104 St. Louise de Marillac Church, Roman Catholic, Upper St. Claire, PA. Architect: Lucian Caste.

105 Rothko Chapel, Interfaith, Houston, TX. Architect: Howard Barnstone. Photographer: Rick Gardner.

106 Unitarian Church, Westport, CT. Architect: Victor Lundy. Photographer: © Cunningham-Werdnigg.

107 Bradford College Helen Bicknell Memorial Chapel, Interfaith, Bradford, MA. Architect: Campbell and Aldrich.

108 Temple Beth El, Bloomfield Township, MI. Architect: Minoru Yamasaki and Associates. Photographer: Balthazar Korab.

109 St. Francis de Sales Church, Roman Catholic, Muskegon, MI. Architect: Marcel Breuer and Herbert Beckhard. Photographer: Donald J. Bruggink.

110 Hartford Seminary Chapel, Interfaith, Hartford, CT. Architect: Richard Meier. Photographer: copyright: Ezra Stoller.

111 North Shore Congregation Israel, Glencoe, IL. Architect: Minoru Yamasaki and Associates. Photographer: Hedrich Blessing.

112 St. Mary's Cathedral, Roman Catholic, San Francisco, CA. Architect: McSweeney, Ryan and Lee. Design Consultant: Pietro Belluschi. Photographer: Morley Baer.

113 Hopewell Baptist Church, Edmond, OK. Architect: Bruce Goff.

114 Sophie and Nathan Gumenick Chapel, Temple Israel, Miami, FL. Architect: Kenneth Treister. Photographer: Bill Maris.

115 Garden Grove Community Church, Garden Grove, CA. Architect: Johnson/Burgee. Photographer: Gordon H. Schenck.

116 Thorncrown Chapel, Interfaith, Eureka Springs, AR. Architect: E. Fay Jones. Photographer: Hursley and Lark.

117 St. Barnabas Church, Episcopal, Greenwich, CT. Architect: Philip Ives.

118 Olivet Lutheran Church, Fargo, ND. Architect: Sovik, Mathre, Sathrum and Quanbeck. Photographer: L.D.J. Spectrum.

119 Northwoods Presbyterian Church, Doraville, GA. Architect: Jack Durham Haynes.

120 Church of St. James the Fisherman, Episcopal, Wellfleet, MA. Architect: Olav Hammarström. Photographer: James Molitor.

121 Baptismal Font, First Baptist Church, Keene, NH. Medium: Bronze. Artist: Silvana Cenci. Architect: Carter and Woodruff. Photographer: Joseph V. Molitor.

122 Le Bien Baptistry, Chapel of the Resurrection, Lutheran, Valparaiso University, Valparaiso, IN. Artist: Helen Hickman, Conrad Schmitt Studios. Architect: Charles Edward Stade and Associates. Liturgical Consultant: Adalbert R. Kretzmann.

123 Baptismal Font, Our Saviour's Lutheran Church, Jackson, MN. Architect: Sovik, Mathre, Sathrum and Quanbeck.

124 Baptismal Font, Saviour Divine Lutheran Church, Palos Hills, IL. Medium: Concrete. Architect: Jaeger, Kupritz. Photographer: William Helmick.

125 Baptismal Font, Christ Church of Hamilton and Wenham, Episcopal. South Hamilton, MA. Medium: Fieldstone. Architect: St. John Smith. Photographer: Mark Sexton.

126 Baptismal Font, Christ Church of Oak Brook, Garden Chapel, Oak Brook, IL. Medium: Terraced Masonry. Artist: C. Edward Ware and Associates. Photographer: Herrlin Studio.

127 Organ, Christ Church of Hamilton and Wenham, Episcopal, South Hamilton, MA. Organ Builder: M.P. Moller Co. Architect: St. John Smith. Photographer: Mark Sexton.

128 Organ, United Church of Christ, Rowayton, CT. Organ Builder: Austin Organ Co. Architect: Joseph Salerno. Photographer: P.E. Guerrero.

129 Organ, Unitarian Society, Hartford, CT. Architect: Victor Lundy. Photographer: Copyright Bruce Cunningham Werdnigg.

130 The Pearl Neugent Nordan antiphonal organ, Trompette en-chamade, National City Christian Church, Disciples of Christ, Washington, DC. Organ Builder: M.P. Moller Co. Architect: John Russell Pope. Photographer: Mattox Photographers.

131 Organ, Trompeta Majestatis (en-chamade reed), The Riverside Church, New York, NY. Organ Builder: Tony Bufano. Sculptor: Jacob Epstein—Christ in Majesty; the original is in Llandaff Cathedral, Cardiff, Wales. Medium: Gold-leafed plaster. Architect: Pelton and Successors.

132 Organ, St. Peter's Lutheran Church, New York, NY. Organ Builder: Johannes Klais Orgelbau, Bonn, Germany. Architect: Hugh Stubbins and Associates.

133 Organ, North Christian Church, Columbus, IN. Organ Builder: Holtkamp Organ Co. Architect: Eero Saarinen and Associates. Photographer: Balthazar Korab.

134 The Holy Spirit, The Roofless Church, Interfaith, New Harmony, IN. Medium: Bronze. Artist: Jacques Lipschitz. Architect: Philip Johnson. Photographer: Copyright, Ezra Stoller.

135 Altar Screen, St. Mark's Episcopal Church, New Canaan, CT. Medium: Bronze. Artist: Clark B. Fitz-Gerald. Architect: Sherwood, Mills and Smith. Photographer: © Cunningham-Werdnigg.

136 Golem, Divine Image, Artist's Collection. Medium: Wood. Artist: Esther Gentle Rattner.

137 Crucifixion, Artist's Collection. Medium: Bronze. Artist: Paolo Soleri. Photographer: Ivan Pintar.